HOW YOU CAN
PRAY
IN THE
END OF DAYS

and my call to
help the pray-ers

by

Dr. Billye Brim

How You Can Pray in the End of Days
and my call to help the pray-ers
by Billye Brim
Paperback ISBN: 978-0-9742156-1-7

Published by
A Glorious Church Fellowship, Inc.
Billye Brim Ministries
Prayer Mountain in the Ozarks
PO Box 40
Branson, MO 65615
(417) 336-4877
www.BillyeBrim.org

Cover Design and Interior Layout by Susan Lofland

CONTENTS

PREFACE

What do I mean by *"The End of Days."*

Very simply: *Things are about to Change!*

We live just before an Age Change.

Technically: the Lord gave Adam a six-day work week to see what man could do in six 1000 years days. We are at the end of the sixth day. (See Chapter 14 of this book.)

God has designed a plan whereby you and I can do important work with Him in this climactic time. And we do it through prayer.

He called me to help the pray-ers.

He gave me an understanding of the times, and even of what we are to do in them.

He charged me to write two books on prayer 35 years ago. This is the first. It may be late. But it could be *right on time!*

—*Billye Brim*

SECTION I

MY PRAYER BIOGRAPHY

CHAPTER 1
The Call

My mother liked to tell this story about me concerning prayer. It happened when I was only three. She and Daddy tucked me into bed every night and listened as I prayed, "Now I lay me down to sleep. I pray the Lord my soul to keep. If I should die before I wake, I pray the Lord my soul to take." Until the night I refused.

"I'm never going to pray that prayer again!" I protested.

Mother was flabbergasted. *She's so young to rebel,* she thought. Until she heard why I refused.

"I can just hear God saying to Jesus, 'Get ready, Jesus. Here comes that same old prayer again.'"

From then on, I made up my own prayers. And I knew that God was listening.

MY EARLY LIFE

My devoted Christian mother grew up in denominational churches. She met my father on a blind date and they were married just a few weeks later. The newlyweds, Willie and Marie, had to keep their marriage secret from June to December 1936. Only her Nazarene mother, Ollie Pearl Hibdon, knew of the marriage. For Marie had to keep her widowed mother's job for her while she recuperated from an operation. It was "depression" days and married women could not hold jobs needed by heads of households.

On weekends Willie Combs came up from the small town of Coweta, Oklahoma to the city of Muskogee to visit his bride. Marie noticed that his behavior was strangely jovial at times. Those times were when he was drinking. Marie had never been around alcohol or an inebriated person.

So, after they moved to the farm they'd bought near Coweta, it was Mother who got Daddy to the spring revival at the First Baptist Church where he gave his heart to the Lord. However, his upbringing had been even more spiritually intense than hers. For he was brought up under the influence of early Pentecostal pioneers. He had just wandered astray in the temptations of what he called, "The Dirty Thirties."

Both Mom and Dad were baptized in water the summer of 1938. And I was technically present, for I was born December 6, 1938.

All their long lives Mom and Dad were faithful to the Lord and to the local church. We were in the First Baptist Church at Coweta every time the doors opened. Sunday morning, Sunday night, Wednesday night, Spring Revival, and Fall Revival.

It was in one of those seasonal revivals that at the age of about seven I was born again. When the evangelist gave the invitation, I walked the aisle, for I had become aware of my need for a Savior; I had been a very naughty girl that week.

That night after church, when we got out of the car at

home, *a feeling of Great Love enveloped me.* As I walked up the hill to the house, I looked up at the stars and said, "Now I belong to Jesus. Now I am saved. Now I am safe. Now I am going to Heaven." And every time I recall my new birth, the "feelings" I experienced that night flood over me again and bring to my remembrance my First Love.

My Call From the Lord

Nurtured in such an environment, with parents and grand-parents who loved me and loved the Lord, I could hear Him when *He called.* As a small child, I knew I was *called* to *speak* to others for Him.

My grandmother in Muskogee lived in an apartment with lots of neighbors. She told me how that when we visited her, even as early as age four I would gather up a crowd of children and preach to them. I led the singing from a leaf off a tree. I took up the offering using a leaf as the offering plate. Then I preached from a leaf I used for the Bible.

> *As a small child, I knew I was called to speak to others for Him.*

Growing up, *the call* was always there. I took part in all kinds of church activities. When I was fourteen or so, I went forward before several thousand people under the big taber-nacle at Falls Creek Baptist Assembly near Davis, Oklahoma, to answer publicly a call to full-time service of the Lord.

Soon after, I remember a night at the First Baptist Church in Broken Arrow, where we then lived. The congregation was singing, *Blessed Assurance.* The Spirit of the Lord came down upon me as we sang the chorus, *"This is my story. This is my song. Praising my Savior all the day long."* A Heavenly Witness assured me that I would praise my Savior all my life long—that I would *speak* for my Savior all my life long.

I tried to find out how to do it. I knew it involved speaking. Teaching. But my denomination, at that time, said that women could not preach. Yet I knew that our women missionaries preached and taught mixed gender congregations in China and Africa. So I read missions books trying to get a call to Africa, but it did not come.

Our family moved to Pryor, Oklahoma when I was a high school Junior. Without seeing how a woman could do it, *the call* faded into the background.

One of my first days at the new school, I noticed a very handsome black-haired, part-Cherokee, Senior who was also a star running back on the football team.

Long story short, I married my high school sweetheart, Kent Brim. And not long after we married, four beautiful children were born to us—two daughters and two sons. Shelli, Terry, and Brenda were born during a time when Kent's work took us to Southern Illinois. Chip was born in Tulsa after we moved back to Oklahoma. At the age of 24, I was the mother of four children under the age of five.

Someone asked Kent, "Are you Catholic?"

"No," He answered. "We are passionate Baptists."

CALLS FROM A FRIEND

We lived in Inola, Oklahoma when I saw an ad in *The Tulsa World:* "Large Stately White House For Sale in Collinsville."

We needed "large" for our family and the Amish girl who stayed during the week to watch the children and the house while I worked. We moved into the 60-year-old, two-story house in August 1964. One day I came home from work and found a note on our dining room table.

Hi, Billye! We live here now! And we'd like to get together with you and Kent.... Pat Martin

We knew the couple from college. With the Martin's five children, and our four, it was lots of noisy fun when we got together. Pat's husband was the football coach. Kent really liked sports. So it was a natural bonding.

In October or November 1966, Pat called me, "You and Kent go to church, don't you? I'd like to go with you. I'd like to sing in the Christmas Cantata. I've never been to church, except for funerals."

It took some doing. But I was a church pianist, so we got her into the choir on short notice for the cantata.

During a church service, Pat accepted the Lord and was born again!

Rather than being glad, I went into a state of conviction. I had not invited her to church; she had to ask me. I had never spoken to her about the Lord in the years we'd known each other.

Then, to add to all that, *the call* rose back up within me, after having been pushed down for years. Kent had no idea, for instance, that he had married a girl with a call of God on her life to preach.

Oh, I still was faithful to church. I played piano and sang.

I led Junior choirs and taught Junior classes. We tithed. But I was so empty.

I remember one night sitting in the car alone weeping. I had read a book about the totally surrendered life of a missionary to China entitled, *Hudson Taylor's Spiritual Secret*. The Holy Spirit was working on me. My heart was melting under the pressure of His persuasion.

That's when another important telephone call came from Pat Martin.

"Do you know what I'm going to do next?" she asked.

"What?"

> *My heart was melting under the pressure of His persuasion.*

"I'm going to receive the baptism with the Holy Spirit and speak with tongues."

"Oh no, you're not!" I said. I had failed to witness to her about the Lord, but I was going to make up for it by keeping her safe.

"That is of the devil!" I practically shouted into the phone.

"Then what is it doing in the Bible?"

"I don't know," I said, "But give me a while and I'll tell you." Pat forced me into scriptures I'd read, but paid little attention to.

I knew nothing about tongues. Nor did I know anything about an outpouring of the Holy Spirit then sweeping around the world called "The Charismatic Move." At that very time, denominational people by the thousands were receiving the experience of the baptism with the Holy Spirit and speaking with other tongues.

A monthly periodical of a major denomination carried an article about it. I did not read the article, but I'd seen the title, emblazoned in large bold print across the top: SPEAKING WITH TONGUES IS OF THE DEVIL. Based on that small bit of misinformation from a writer who knew no more than I did about the subject, I told Pat that speaking with tongues was of the devil.

A CALL FROM THE DOCTOR'S WIFE

Another telephone call came. It was from Allie Huneryager, the wife of a local physician, Dr. Lloyd Huneryager. She asked if she could visit me. I didn't really know her, though I had seen the Huneryager's at church. And Kent had told me about a man in his Sunday School class who usually took it over. He said the teacher would open and soon thereafter, Dr. Huneryager would comment on the lesson.

I straightened up my house and got ready for someone so high on the social scale, *I thought,* of our small town of 2500.

I can almost still see Allie standing at my door as I answered it. She was tall and slender of build. But she was not standing tall and straight. Her posture was off balance. With both hands she tightly grasped the handle of the heavy Wollensack recorder propped against her upper leg, bent at the knee.

She came right in and plopped the recorder with a thud on my coffee table.

"I came to play a tape for you," she said.

What does that mean? I thought.

It was April 1967—BC: before cassettes, even.

She proceeded to wind the 7-inch reel tape around the spindle and pressed *Play*. Then she sat completely silent as the reels began to turn.

A man's voice, very Texan in accent, filled the room. I learned later his name was Kenneth E. Hagin. The tape was his recorded message entitled, "The Father's Care." Based on the Lord's own prayer in John 17, it was all about how much God loves us and cares for us.

Kenneth Hagin read how Jesus prayed to the Father, "And You have loved them as You have loved Me" (John 17:23).

Brother Hagin emphasized that verse saying, "God loves us as much as He loves Jesus."

I wept. I was literally sitting down on the floor next to the coffee table sobbing. My already Holy Ghost softened heart, absolutely melted.

Mrs. Huneryager moved right in for the kill.

"Mrs. Brim," she said. "Before you try to convince Mrs. Martin that the baptism with the Holy Spirit is of the devil, don't you think you should know more about it?"

"I really should," I blubbered through my tears.

"This man is teaching a seminar on the subject next week in Tulsa. I would like to take you and Mrs. Martin as my guests."

Now I knew where Mrs. Martin was getting her information.

That next week my life changed forever. And I began to see that I could answer *the call*.

Chapter 2

Brim Full of the Holy Ghost

Since I was not working outside my home at the time, I was free to join a happy group of four ladies traveling daily to Tulsa for Kenneth Hagin's ten-day seminar on The Holy Spirit.

Twice daily on weekdays, and once on Sunday, Allie Huneryager picked up Pat Martin, Ranona Standridge (another friend whose husband was a deacon in our church) and me, and we drove about 20 miles south to 1029 North Utica in Tulsa. Evangelists T. L. and Daisy Osborne had moved into larger quarters and had sold the building to Kenneth Hagin Ministries for their new headquarters.

Kenneth E. Hagin's Vision
The River of Praise

Kenneth E. Hagin had only recently moved from Texas to Tulsa at the leading of the Lord. Part of his leading came in the form of a vision he saw in 1962, and which he called, "The River of Praise." Here is how he described it:

> ...I saw a beautiful flower garden...with a white picket fence around it...overgrown with flowers...glorious...

indescribable...no words could tell of its beauty. Such an aroma went up from these flowers that the fragrance seemed to be multiplied a hundredfold, forming a cloud of incense...When I reached the gate, Jesus was there to open it for me....

To the west I saw flowing into the garden what looked like a river. It narrowed where it came into the garden. Then it seemed to become wider and wider, rising into the sky... The River appeared to be pouring tons of water into the garden.

Then the water changed and...instead of a river of water, it was a river of people! I saw men with silk top hats and long-tailed coats and women in evening gowns. I saw businessmen in smartly tailored suits. I saw laborers and housewives with their work clothes...I saw people of all sorts—all of them singing praises as they flowed into the garden.

Then the Lord said to me, "These people...are what you call 'denominational people' or denominations other than Full Gospel. In this day, I am visiting hungry hearts everywhere. Wherever I find hearts that are open to Me, in whatever church they may be, I will visit them in this hour. I also will visit places you never would have thought I would visit—not only what you call 'denominational churches,' but I also will visit other religions where hearts are hungry and open to Me. I will bring them into full salvation and into the baptism of the Holy Spirit.

"This river is...people who will be called in these last days and who will flow as one and will come together as one. The beautiful aroma of these flowers is the praise of these people ascending into Heaven, even as the incense of old ascended unto me.

"You must play a part in this. You will work with these people in the various denominations. You will minister to Full Gospel people to help them be prepared for My coming. I will show you how and what to do."[1]

THE WORD ON THE SPIRIT

I did not know then, but I know now, that we were part of that river. Brother Hagin was told by the Lord that he must meet us on neutral ground. The small room we walked into that day, which was converted from office space, held about 150 people. And it was jam-packed.

Down front seats were hard to get. I had never seen such a scramble to sit at the front. In our church it was the back that was crowded. But Allie marched us down to the front row to reserved seats. I did not realize that the Huneryager's were on Brother Hagin's board of directors.

The atmosphere was exhilarating. The music was Spirit-filled. Brother Hagin's son-in-law, Buddy Harrison, led the spirited singing. Sarah Borrell's fingers ran up and down the keyboard of the old upright piano with a Pentecostal anointing—though at the time I would not have known to call it that. And, if anyone had mentioned to me that Kenneth Hagin was a prophet who saw visions, I would have run out of the building.

Kenneth Hagin was 49, tall and slim. He had as guest speakers Reverend and Mrs. J. R. Goodwin, longtime pastors at the First Assembly of God Church in Pasadena, Texas. There was a purity, a dignity, a holiness about Kenneth and Oretha Hagin, and J. R. and Carmen Goodwin.

Every morning, in the calm speaking voice of a teacher, Brother Hagin went through the Bible, particularly the New Testament, and scripture by scripture expounded on what the Word of God says about the Holy Spirit in the new birth, and in the baptism with the Holy Spirit with the evidence of speaking with other tongues.

Some of the very lessons I heard are published in Kenneth E. Hagin's book, TONGUES BEYOND THE UPPER ROOM: *Everything you want to know about speaking in tongues.*[2]

My Questions Answered

I listened intently. I had been brought up believing in the integrity of the Word of God. So when I heard what the Word said, by day five, I was convinced. Especially after Brother Hagin answered a question that had been forming in my mind.

We were told that on Friday, we could ask questions. I could hardly wait to ask mine and I was the first to shoot up my hand.

My question, carefully thought out, was: *If you are born again, and you are right with God, and you see that this is a gift, and you don't receive—what could be stopping you from receiving this baptism?*

You see, I had been going home after the sessions and asking the Lord to baptize me with the Holy Spirit with no results.

Brother Hagin spent the entire session answering my question. The answer was so wonderful. To this day I consider this information of utmost value to one desiring this wonderful gift from God.

Brother Hagin said, "Either one of two things could be hindering you. And they are: (1) A lack of faith, or (2) A lack of yielding.

"If it is a lack of faith, then you go back over the scriptures on the subject until faith arises in your heart. For faith comes by hearing, and hearing by the Word of God (Romans 10:17). Everything from God, from the New Birth on, is received by faith.

"But nine times out of ten, it is not a lack of faith that hinders, but a lack of yielding."

And Brother Hagin taught the rest of the session on how to yield to the Holy Spirit. He said that this is of primary importance in living an overcoming life in God. Throughout life we must know how to yield to the Spirit of God.

I got it!

And following that morning session, Pat, Ranona, and I went into a small room at the back (that room would become my office three years later). There Kenneth and Oretha Hagin laid hands on us and prayed for us to be filled with the Holy Spirit. And we were!

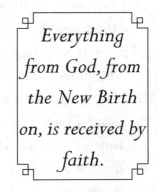

Everything from God, from the New Birth on, is received by faith.

I literally went off like a fountain! Divinely given words bubbled up from my spirit with a force. Beautiful words flowed out my mouth in a language, or languages, unknown to me.

Pat Martin later said, "I don't think it's fair. I only received a couple of words. And I have believed in this longer than you have."

"Yes," I said. "But you weren't born again 20 years without this second experience in the Holy Spirit—your spirit knowing that there was a further experience and waiting for it."

When I learned how to yield to the Spirit, I recognized that many times before in my life, He had come upon me just like He did that April 1967 day. For example: The night I was born again. At Falls Creek camp. In many services at the churches I grew up in. So many times I had walked forward to rededicate my life because of the Spirit's moving upon me. And if I had only known how to yield to Him, I could have spoken in tongues with all its benefits many years earlier.

For days I spoke and sang in tongues. Those spring days in 1967 were so filled with light. The flowers were brighter—their aroma more fragrant. The song of the birds was sweeter. It was the most beautiful spring I'd ever known.

This flow has not subsided now for 48 years. Long ago, Brother J. R. Goodwin called me, "Brim full of the Holy Ghost." May that appellation apply to me all the days of my life!

But let's go on with the meeting that 1967 spring. For we did not realize then what all was happening on the very night we first heard a prophetic word through Sister Clara Grace. And only of late have we discovered that this included a sign of the times in the heavens.

---

1. Kenneth E. Hagin, *I Believe in Visions*, (Tulsa, OK: RHEMA BIBLE CHURCH, aka Kenneth Hagin Ministries, 1984), pp 115-117.

2. Ibid. *TONGUES BEYOND THE UPPER ROOM*, (2007).

CHAPTER 3

A PROPHETIC MEETING

O n Saturday, I called Mother with the good news! It didn't take long to realize that it wasn't good news to her. She had probably read the same headline I had quoted to Pat Martin that speaking with tongues was of the devil. It was Daddy who was from the Pentecostal side of the family. Mother's background was denominational.

I quickly began to appease her, "Oh, Mother. It's in the Word. I'll show you when I see you. I'm going to go along with these Pentecostals where I see they are right. But I promise you I won't go along with any of their error. I won't wash off all my make-up, or let my hair grow long and wear it in a bun. *And I promise you, I won't listen to any women preachers.*"

(Allow me to say here that I think people should live their convictions. Some very spiritual people I have known through the years don't wear make-up, etc., and it would have gone against their convictions to do so. Yet we enjoyed close spiritual fellowship. They accepted me, short hair, lipstick and all. My remarks to Mother that day simply tell you where I was then.

(I fondly recall what happened one night after a glorious

meeting in Washington D.C. where I was invited to speak by a 90-year-old, or so, old-time Pentecostal woman preacher. All the leaders and musicians had long hair, long skirts, and faces free of paint. The musical group literally led us to the very throne of God. One night after services, we had a pajama party of sorts. The leader of the oh-so-anointed musicians, laughed as she told us of how shocked she was, and I quote, "The first time I heard the Word of the Lord coming through painted lips—and I knew it was the Word of the Lord.")

A WOMAN PREACHER!

You can imagine my surprise when we arrived on the second Monday night, and Kenneth Hagin introduced the speaker, Clara Grace. A woman! A 75-year-old woman preacher. And not only that, I learned later she was a prophetess!

> *That's the best sermon I ever heard. And she's out of order.*

But, to my amazement, the atmosphere was charged, filled with God. The anointing—now I know to call it that—was strong. You could "feel" it. Every word she or Brother Hagin uttered penetrated my being with Holy Spirit power.

I remember thinking, *That's the best sermon I ever heard. And she's out of order.*

I went on with my reasoning, *But maybe at the judgment seat of Christ, she will be on a level with all the men preachers who were not so good.*

You see, somewhere in the back of my mind I'd always

felt that if I did preach, I would get in trouble at the judgment seat of Christ.

Yet to tell you the real truth, that night, I did not have a clue as to what she was saying. It was the prophetic anointing that so impacted me.

It was eleven years later, when I was the editor of publications at Kenneth Hagin Ministries that the Lord directed me to go back into the archives and, "Find out what she said." I'm sure He impressed me to do this only after I had grown enough to receive it.

So I did. I got the cassette tape. By then progress had been made and our tape department had transferred the reel tapes to cassettes.

As I listened with rapt attention, it was as if I heard the meeting for the first time.

A Prophetic Message

Clara Grace opened with a prayer that I can now see was answered. Here are parts of it:

> ...So come, O Father. Jesus manifest Thyself tonight. And meet the need of hungry hearts (tongues) who are here, who have come [KEH in background, Yes!] from these distant places...Let Thy will be done in every life....

The entire message was prophetic. But this stood out:

> God is preparing a special core of people, a special breed of men! AND women!!! [KEH, Amen!]...He is preparing a special people to do a special thing in

the Body of Christ. That's why you're here from Minneapolis. That's why you're here from California. That's why you're here from Dallas. That's why...

(And then it was as if she heard the Lord say something.) What is it?

It's a gathering of the chiefs of God's army. Oh, I didn't mean to say that. **Of the chiefs of the clan.** Hallelujah! [KEH, Hallelujah!]

"It's a gathering of the chiefs of... the clan."

I sometimes jokingly say that if you had been there, and heard the word that those people were some of the chiefs of the clan, you would have been excused for doubting it. For it didn't look like a meeting of chiefs. We were mostly denominational people, writing in our Bibles for the first time. And that was only because Brother Hagin told us we could do it. Even then, at first I underlined the scriptures almost with fear and trembling.

But I look back now knowing how God has used some of those people who were in that seminar. Phil and Fern Halverson. Vicki Jameson. Reverend Harley Fiddler. Jeanne Wilkerson. Lowell and Bobbie Furry. Buddy and Pat Harrison. Kenneth and Gloria Copeland. And others....

The Copelands came there in their worn out car. Ken was a freshman at ORU. It was about that time that he asked Buddy Harrison if he could leave the car at the ministry in exchange for Kenneth Hagin's tapes. Buddy told him to take the tapes, but please don't leave the car.

Now I was there, but not from far away distance wise, only 20 miles north. Yet it took the Lord's strong dealings to get me there spiritually.

Gloria Copeland and I have talked so many times about how grateful we are that the Lord got us there. Almost every BVOV television broadcast we somehow get around to reminiscing and thanking the Lord for being in those life-changing meetings.

I remember a word of prophecy through Kenneth E. Hagin to Kenneth Copeland several years later. The Lord said that He had maneuvered Ken as one maneuvers a ship into a harbor. Thank God, I was among those maneuvered to be in that meeting that spring of 1967.

A VISION OF THE GLORIOUS CHURCH

Clara Grace was released to share a vision with our little group that night. It had come several years before when she attended a meeting hosted by John Osteen. Kenneth Hagin was a speaker. The following is taken from the account of the vision she gave us.

> He [Kenneth Hagin] was speaking the last Friday morning... When he was near the close, suddenly, he veered off...and began talking about science in relationship to the advance of the church. And to the fact that God would not allow one phase of His program to outstrip the other... And he said, "You know, science entered the realm of spirit when they discovered the place of timelessness...."

> And when Brother Hagin said this, all I know to say is, I left there—I was in the Spirit. I was not conscious of anybody. I never knew one thing going on around me for I was in the Spirit....
>
> But I do know this! He opened the heavens to me. He rolled them back like great curtains, like great scrolls. And it was only a thin veil. There was only a thin veil between me and the *Glory*. I could see the *Glory*, but it was behind the veil.

Without going into the very long vision, suffice it to say; she saw a vision comparable to Tommy Hicks' vision. In both, the *Glory* of the Lord moved upon a struggling Body of Christ, strengthening and preparing it to walk in the very last days before His Coming as *The Glorious Church.*

And without our knowledge then—and I only became aware of it, just a short time ago—a rare event occurred in the heavens in the early morning hours of April 24, 1967.

CHAPTER 4

BLOOD MOONS

I am sure scientifically minded people around the world observed the blood moon eclipse of April 24, 1967.

I am almost as sure that the 150 or so people in that meeting with Clara Grace were oblivious to it.

And I am surer still that even those scientifically minded people who did watch it, and who knew it was the first blood moon in a tetrad, had not the slightest inkling of its spiritual significance.

I would venture to say that almost no one on earth knew the Creator had arranged for a sign in the heavens of the events about to take place in Israel—the events of the miraculous Six-Day War.

I certainly knew nothing about the eclipse. In fact, I did not even know that the evening of April 24, 1967 was the evening of Passover *(Pesach).* Nor did I know that Jews all over the world were celebrating the traditional Seder meal that the Lord told Israel to observe forever (Exodus 12:24).

GOD'S CALENDAR

Of course, after the Lord, in the 1970s, made clear to me

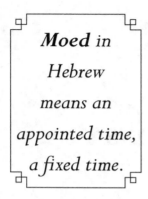

Moed in *Hebrew* means an appointed time, *a fixed time.*

the part of my call that is to Israel... And then when He sent me to Israel to "study Hebrew in the Land" in the 1980s... During my learning process, I learned about God's calendar which He revealed in Leviticus 23, and which He charged Israel to keep.

The Jews have faithfully kept the seven *moeds* (appointed times) on that prophetic calendar: Passover *(Pesach),* Feast of Unleavened Bread, First Fruits, Pentecost *(Shavuot),* Trumpets, Day of Atonement, and Tabernacles *(Sukkot).*

What is a *moed?*

Moed in Hebrew means *an appointed time, a fixed time.*

The first mention of the word in the Bible is in the account of the creations of the fourth day:

> **Gen. 1:14** And God said, Let there be lights in the firmament of the heaven to divide the day from the night; and let them be for signs, and for seasons, and for days, and years:
> **Gen. 1:15** And let them be for lights in the firmament of the heaven to give light upon the earth: and it was so.
> **Gen. 1:16** And God made two great lights; the greater light to rule the day, and the lesser light to rule the night: *he made* the stars also.

The word translated "seasons" in verse 14 is *moeds* in the original Hebrew. The sun, the moon, and the stars are for *signs* and for *moeds.*

God is a sign-giving God.

Moeds are the appointed dates on God's calendar—the significant dates He has circled on His prophetic calendar of redemption. The days set apart from all other days in the year. The holy days. Therefore, holidays.

We see the word again in Leviticus 23 where God delineates that calendar and its *moeds.* In the following verses I have inserted the word *moed* where a form of it is used in the original Hebrew text:

> **Lev. 23:2** Speak unto the children of Israel, and say unto them, *Concerning* the feasts *[moeds]* of the LORD, which ye shall proclaim *to be* holy convocations, *even* these *are* my feasts *[moeds].*

> **Lev. 23:4** These *are* the feasts *[moeds]* of the LORD, *even* holy convocations, which ye shall proclaim in their seasons *[moeds].*
> **Lev. 23:5** In the fourteenth *day* of the first month at even *is* the LORD'S passover....

Consider the following substantiating verse concerning the moon and *moeds*:

> **Psa. 104:19** He appointed the moon for seasons *[moeds]....*

BLOOD MOON TETRADS

But it was 2009, or so, before I just happened to hear about blood moon tetrads, and the extreme rarity of their occurring on the *moeds* of God's calendar.

I first heard about them on Reverend J.R. Church's television program, *Prophecy in the News.* I vaguely knew of

J.R. Church; but I could count on the fingers of one hand how many times I'd watched the broadcast. On the episode I just happened to see, a Pastor Mark Biltz was visibly excited as he shared about his then recent discovery. The following excerpt is from his introduction to a book he published in 2014, but it iterates what he shared on Church's broadcast:

> ...in 2008, something radical happened. In March...I saw on the Internet an incredible total lunar eclipse over the Temple Mount in Jerusalem. I had read all the Bible verses in Isaiah, Joel, the Gospels, and Revelation...about the moon turning to blood and the sun to sackcloth. I began to ponder the possibilities of tying the eclipses mentioned...to the coming of the Messiah.
>
> Because I love science and astronomy, I decided to look into the future occurrences of eclipses. I remembered that NASA has a list of eclipses that covers five thousand years...I noticed...four total lunar eclipses in a row for 2014 and 2015. I noted their dates on our calendar....
>
> One morning, as I was praying, a thought popped into my head: *Why don't I compare the dates of the eclipses on the NASA website to the dates on the biblical calendar?* ...I was shocked to find that all four eclipses—over both years—fell on the biblical holidays of Passover and the Feast of Tabernacles....
>
> I...pulled up NASA's website to look up other times when there have been four consecutive blood moons, which are total lunar eclipses, where the moon appears blood red. NASA calls four total blood moons in a row a *tetrad,* and they list their occurrences. I noticed there weren't any in the 1600s, 1700s, or even the 1800s. The last time there was a tetrad was back in the 1900s, and to my amazement,

they also fell on the feasts of Passover and Tabernacles.

When I noticed the years these phenomena occurred, my mind began reeling. The last two times there were four blood moons in a row, they happened, first, right after Israel became a nation in 1948, and then again when Israel retook Jerusalem in 1967.[1]

Thousands of people learned of blood moon tetrads on God's *moeds* with the publishing in 2013 of Pastor John Hagee's New York Times best-selling book *Four Blood Moons: Something is About to Change.*[2] In a television interview Pastor Hagee said:

> "There's a sense in the world that things are changing and God is trying to communicate with us in a supernatural way," Hagee told CBN News. "This is too much to be a happenstance."

Like these ministers, and many others, I have researched NASA and other sites studying eclipses. I have also studied God's calendar and its *moeds.* You can see what I've learned about the latter in our publications, *The Book of Daniel Syllabus* and *The Book of Revelation Syllabus.*[3] In my study of eclipses, the following is some of what I have learned:

"This is too much to be a happenstance."

- Lunar eclipses occur on average twice a year.
- There are 3 types: penumbral, partial, total.

- They usually occur in no particular order.
- An orderly sequence of 4 total eclipses with no others between is called a tetrad.
- During the period 1600 to 1900 there were no tetrads at all.
- During the 21st Century, 9 sets of tetrads occur.

Tetrads are rare. But what is extremely rare is a tetrad of eclipses occurring on the Jewish Feast dates—the God-marked *moeds* on His calendar. The three times these rare heavenly signs have appeared on those dates, they have marked a period of world-changing events connected to Israel. Here they are:

Passover and Tabernacles 1493 and 1494
1. Passover (Pesach) – April 2, 1493
2. Tabernacles (Sukkot) – September 25, 1493
3. Passover (Pesach) – March 22, 1494
4. Tabernacles (Sukkot) – September 15, 1494

After years of torture and murder during the long years of the Spanish Inquisition, the Jews were robbed of their belongings and kicked out of Spain in the summer of 1492.
At exactly the same time, Columbus sailed, eventually discovering a New World and a resting place for Jews until they would return to their Promised Land.

Passover and Tabernacles 1949 and 1950
1. Passover (Pesach) – April 13, 1949
2. Tabernacles (Sukkot) – October 7, 1949
3. Passover (Pesach) – April 2, 1950
4. Tabernacles (Sukkot) – September 26, 1950

The State of Israel was reborn in May 1948. Israel's fledgling fighting forces were extremely outnumbered by the armies of the Arab states who attacked them. Yet Israel's War of Independence ended in victory in 1949. According to the dry bones prophecy, Israel had come up out of the graves of the Holocaust (Ezekiel 37). The first Passover celebrated by the Old-New State in her ancient Promised Land was marked by the start of a blood moon tetrad.

Passover and Tabernacles 1967 and 1968
1. Passover (Pesach) – April 24, 1967
2. Tabernacles (Sukkot) – October 18, 1967
3. Passover (Pesach) – April 13, 1968
4. Tabernacles (Sukkot) – October 6, 1968

This tetrad marked the season of the miraculous Six-Day War and its dramatic outcome. Israel regained the Old City of Jerusalem, the Western Wall, the Temple Mount. They were again possessors of the places where their ancient ancestors lived and worshipped.

Passover and Tabernacles 2014 and 2015
1. Passover (Pesach) – April 15, 2014
2. Tabernacles (Sukkot) – October 8, 2014
3. Passover (Pesach) – April 4, 2015
4. Tabernacles (Sukkot) – September 28, 2015

And now, as I write in the spring of 2015, we are in the midst of the tetrad Mark Biltz discovered. World-shaking events in the Middle East are changing its very face. And we little know what all is really happening on the grander scale of *the end of days.*

SOLAR ECLIPSES ON TWO NEW YEAR'S DAYS

Since ancient times Jews have kept two main calendars: a civic year, and a sacred year. The civic calendar is the older. It begins with Rosh Hashana in the autumn and counts time from the creation of Adam. The keeping of the sacred calendar, was commanded by the LORD the night they came out of Egypt, the night of the first Passover *(Pesach)*. The sacred calendar begins in the biblical month of Aviv, Hebrew for spring (Exodus 34:18). This month is now called Nissan.

> **Ex. 12:1** And the LORD spake unto Moses and Aaron in the land of Egypt, saying,
>
> **Ex. 12:2** This month *shall* be unto you the beginning of months: it *shall* be the first month of the year to you.
>
> **Ex. 12:3** Speak ye unto all the congregation of Israel, saying, In the tenth *day* of this month they shall take to them every man a lamb, according to the house of *their* fathers, a lamb for an house:...
>
> **Ex. 12:6** And ye shall keep it up until the fourteenth day of the same month: and the whole assembly of the congregation of Israel shall kill it in the evening.
>
> **Ex. 12:7** And they shall take of the blood, and strike *it* on the two side posts and on the upper door post of the houses, wherein they shall eat it.
>
> **Ex. 12:8** And they shall eat the flesh in that night, roast with fire, and unleavened bread; *and* with bitter *herbs* they shall eat it...
>
> **Ex. 12:11** And thus shall ye eat it; *with* your loins girded, your shoes on your feet, and your staff in your hand; and ye shall eat it in haste: it *is* the LORD'S passover.

Solar eclipses mark the first days of both calendar years that begin during the span of the blood moon tetrad of 2014 and 2015.

An extremely rare total solar eclipse could be seen in the

far north regions of Earth on the first day of the sacred calendar year, the 1st of the Hebrew month of Nissan. The Gre-
gorian calendar date is Friday, March 20, 2015.

> *Root Source's* co-founder, Bob O'Dell, a Christian
> who has studied lunar and solar astronomical
> events for more than 35 years, discovered that two
> weeks before the Passover Blood Moon [April 4,
> 2015], an exceedingly rare solar eclipse will be tak-
> ing place. There will be a total eclipse of the sun for
> two minutes over the North Pole on Friday, March
> 20, the day of the Spring Equinox which coincides
> with the beginning of the Hebrew month of Nissan,
> the first month in the Biblical calendar year, a solar
> occurrence that has never happened before in
> human history.
>
> "The occurrence and rarity of this natural event,
> together with the times in which we live, indicates
> the finger of God," said Gidon Ariel, an Israeli Ortho-
> dox Jew and co-founder of *Root Source.* A total solar
> eclipse at the North Pole on the first day of spring
> occurs once every 100,000 years.... [4]

Rosh Hashana is the first day of the civil year. In 2015 Rosh
Hashana begins the evening of September 13. A partial solar
eclipse occurs on that date.

Now, Back to Tulsa on April 24, 1967

That night in Tulsa, April 24, 1967, was a night of far greater prophetic significance than anyone present in Kenneth
Hagin's seminar on the Holy Spirit could have imagined.

Did things change in the world?

Monumentally!

Did things change in my life? And in the lives of other ministers who were there?

Prodigiously and Forever! Though it took some time to realize how much.

---

1. Mark Biltz, *Blood Moons,* (Washington, D.C.: WND Books, 2014), pp xvi, xvii.

2. John Hagee, *Four Blood Moons, Something is About to Change,* (Brentwood, TN: Worthy Publishing, 2013).

3. Dr. Billye Brim, *The Book of Daniel, Syllabus,* Time: God's Calendar, *Moeds,* pp 79-86; Time: Shmittah Cycles and the Jubilee, pp 87-89, *The Book of Revelation, Syllabus,* Time: *Moeds,* pp 96-103; Time: Shmittah Cycles and The Jubilee, pp 104-105. (Branson, MO: Billye Brim Ministries).

4. Gidon Ariel and Bob O'Dell, *BLOOD MOONS 101,* Root Source. (http://root-source.com/blood-moons-101).

Chapter 5

Moving in the Spirit

*A*nd Jesus being full of the Holy Ghost...was led by the Spirit... (Luke 4:1).

That's just what happened to us in 1967.

At first, right after I was filled with the Spirit, we were led to be in every Holy Ghost meeting we could get to.

The Huneryager's took us to hear Dr. Hilton Sutton every time that anointed prophecy teacher from Texas was anywhere near. It was thrilling to hear him throughout his long life, but it was especially exhilarating to hear him the year Israel got back Jerusalem. Through his teachings, the Lord awakened me to what was happening in Israel and the nations, and that the coming of the Lord was on the horizon.

We particularly went to every seminar Kenneth E. Hagin held in his office building where I had first met the Holy Spirit in a new dimension.

I would call out to the children, ages 4, 6, 8, and 9, "Come in and get cleaned up. We are going to church tonight."

"Which one?" they would ask. "Our church, or the Praise the Lord Church?"

That pretty well explains a difference that existed.

Moved to Cajun Country

Then, perhaps to change me, to free me from religiosity, the Spirit moved us to Baton Rouge, Louisiana. We thought it was Kent's work that was taking him there; and we decided we would move as a family before school started in the fall.

The summer of 1967, the Huneryager's also took us to FGBMFI meetings. That long acronym stands for the long name of an organization the Lord used mightily to bring people together and into the baptism with the Holy Spirit, in those exciting days of The Charismatic Move. Full Gospel Business Men's Fellowship International was divinely planted in the heart of Demos Shakarian. And I highly recommend his book, *The Happiest People on Earth.*[1]

We went to an FGBMFI banquet in Tulsa just before we moved to Louisiana. The speaker was a physician from Baton Rouge, Dr. Jere Melilli, Sr.

After the meeting, I went up to him and asked, "Do you know of a good Baptist church we could go to in Baton Rouge?"

"Oh, yes," he replied. And he recommended Bethany Baptist Church in Baker.

The Move of the Spirit at Bethany

We moved to Baton Rouge in August of 1967 and soon after, we drove out Plank Road and found the sign: Bethany Baptist Church. (The Baptist was later dropped.)

Today Bethany has thousands of members, huge campuses, and churches around the world. But then, it was small.

Just a seed of what would come. But that little seed was alive, like a Mexican jumping bean. And I do mean *jumping*.

Pastor Roy Stockstill had led a large denominational church in Baton Rouge, when he received the baptism with the Holy Spirit during the Charismatic Move. He stepped away from that pastorate, and just four years before we got there, he started a small non-denominational church in Bethany.

When we found the place, the building itself was comparatively small. But in the years we were there from 1967 to 1970, there was a constant need for more room, and an ongoing building program.

> *But that little seed was alive, like a Mexican jumping bean.*

Now back to the *jumping*.

I recently met Pastor Larry Stockstill, Roy's son, at an Awakening America Alliance meeting we both attended. Larry and I, and two others with him, who were at Bethany when we were there, reminisced about the praise and worship in those early days.

In all the years since, and I have been in hundreds of worship services, I have NEVER seen the anointing we experienced every service at Bethany.

As I remember it, a rather sober-faced organist took her place at the instrument. But the moment her hands dropped to the keyboard, the Holy Ghost fell! Every time!

Two people stand out in my memory. Wind-Mill Prophet and Twirley-Bird. Wind-Mill would move around the front with the music, swooping with his arms like a wind-mill.

It's been a long time ago, but it seems to me his eyes were closed. Twirley-Bird was a diminutive lady who spun like a top. Sometimes until she dropped!

The entire congregation ascended together to the heights in worship. And it wasn't somber. It was filled with joy and life!

I particularly remember watching Brother Roy's wife, Ruth. Eyes closed, hands lifted, her face seemed to light up, especially when we sang the hymn, "Higher Ground."

The nine gifts of the Holy Spirit operated at Bethany.

> *The entire congregation ascended together to the heights in worship.*

I remember one time in particular. And to tell you the truth, I was what might be called a little "back-slidden." You see, it was the first time in my life I had lived in a city. From childhood, I'd lived in small towns where everyone knew who I was, and who my parents were. So, since I was working at the time, when we first got to Baton Rouge, I fell into the habit of skipping church. No one would know. And other things....

One rainy morning driving to work, I entered an intersection too soon, and a car going too fast took the motor off the front of my car. The hand of God kept me alive. Shaken but unscratched, I called Kent who was at home that morning. I was worried because it could have been my fault and I didn't have a Louisiana driver's license. He and the children made a circle and praised God for my safety, asking Him to intervene on my behalf. Their prayer was answered.

The very next Sunday, I got my family and myself to church. The moment I walked into the classroom, the Sunday School teacher visibly reacted at seeing me.

She said, "When I was combing my hair and looking into the mirror this week, I saw your face. And I prayed for you. I also prayed that you would be here today."

We hadn't been going there long enough for her even to know my name. The Holy Ghost had alerted her to pray.

There is too much to tell about our time in Baton Rouge, but Bethany took much of the religiosity out of me.

MOVED BACK TO OKLAHOMA

After our three years there, the next place M.W. Kellogg had work for Kent was in Pennsylvania. I wanted to go with him, but he thought it would be better for the children for us to move back to our home in Collinsville. He said he was sure work would open up again in Oklahoma, and he would get back as soon as he could. I was adamant against it.

One Sunday night, we'd had company, and were late heading to church, so we stopped at a closer church with which Bethany had good fellowship. They were in special meetings. The song service was going when we walked in. The visiting minister, who did not know us, stopped the music, and walked straight back and stood in front of Kent and began to prophesy, "You have the plan of the Lord."

So, the children and I moved back into the stately white house in Collinsville, that we bought after I saw the ad in *The Tulsa World*.

But I missed Kent. After the children went to school, I was

lonely. So, I looked in the want ads of that same newspaper and saw the ad: "Wanted: Part-time Bookkeeper, Spirit-filled. 3 days a week. 1029 North Utica."

Why that's Brother Hagin's place, I thought.

Long story short, I got the job.

---

1. Demos Shakarian as told to John and Elizabeth Sherrill, *The Happiest People on Earth*, (Fleming H. Revell, 1979).

CHAPTER 6

PLACED BY THE SPIRIT

When I came to apply for the job, I saw that Kenneth Hagin Ministries in Tulsa was growing. In April 1967, when Allie Huneryager took me to that life-changing meeting, they had a staff of four—Kenneth and Oretha Hagin, their daughter, Pat Harrison, and her husband, Buddy. The family lived upstairs, over the downstairs offices.

When I was hired in 1970, I was employee number twelve. The Hagin's and the Harrison's had moved into homes. And the upstairs apartments had been changed into offices.

My position as part-time bookkeeper lasted only a few weeks. For an unusual chain of events propelled me into another position.

To understand what happened, you need to know about Kenneth E. Hagin and His call.

"GO TEACH MY PEOPLE FAITH"

Kenneth E. Hagin was born prematurely at home in 1917. Weighing less than two pounds, his survival was a miracle. He grew up sickly with a deformed heart and multiple blood diseases. At 15 he became bedfast and lay partially paralyzed for 16 months.

His amazing experiences during those months include: Dying three times, and descending to the very gates of hell. Being born again. Dying again—and this time ascending toward heaven. Hearing a Voice sending him back.

After this, he asked for a Bible. His grandmother propped a Bible in front of him. At first, he could read only 10 minutes a day, so he started with the New Testament, beginning with Matthew. After a long time, he came to the verse that eventually brought him off what he called "the bed of affliction."

He said that light entered the darkness when he first read, Mark 11:24, *"Therefore I say unto you, What things soever ye desire, when ye pray, believe that ye receive them, and ye shall have them."*

After a long time, and much struggle with the verse and its meaning, the following happened.

> In this moment, I saw exactly what that verse in Mark 11:24 meant. Until then I was going to wait until I was actually healed before I believed I had received my healing. I was looking at my body and testing my heartbeat to see if I had been healed. But I saw that the verse says you have to believe *when* you pray. The *having* comes after the *believing.* I had been reversing it. I was trying to *have* first, and then *believe* second....
>
> "I see it. I see it!" I said with joy. "I see what I've got to do, Lord. I've got to believe that my heart is well while I'm still lying here on this bed, and while my heart is not beating right. I've got to believe that my paralysis is gone while I'm still lying here helpless....
>
> "I believe in my heart that You have heard my

prayer! I believe that my heart is healed and that my paralysis is gone! I believe in my heart that I have received healing for my body!"

As I said this, the thought came to me, "You're a pretty thing. Just look at you, claiming to be a Christian and now you've started lying. Don't you know the Bible says that all liars will have their part in the lake that burneth with fire and brimstone?"

"I am not a liar," I declared.

"Certainly you are, because you said you are healed and you're not."

"I didn't say that I am healed because I feel like it," I stated. "I'm healed because I believe it. And, devil, if you say I am not, then you are a liar. I am acting on the Word of God. If I am not healed, then Jesus is a liar. Go argue with God about it; don't fuss with me."

> *"I didn't say that I am healed because I feel like it. I'm healed because I believe it."*

With this, the devil left me alone. Then I said, "Thank God, I'm healed." I lifted my hands and praised God.

Momentarily, I started to feel my heart to see if it was beating normally, but I caught myself and stated that I wasn't going by feelings but by faith. I kept saying that my heart was well. I praised the Lord in this manner for about 10 minutes.

Then the Holy Spirit spoke as an inner witness on the inside of me and said, "You believe you are healed. If you are healed, then you should be up and out of that bed. Well people are up at 10:00 in the morning."

...I pushed myself up to a sitting position with my hands. Then I reached down, got hold of my feet, and swung them around to the side of the bed. I couldn't feel them, but I could see them. Then I said that I was going to stand and walk.

The devil fought me every inch of the way....

I got ahold of the bedpost and pulled myself up to a standing position. The room started spinning...I closed my eyes, wrapped my arms around the bedpost, and stood there for a few minutes. Finally I opened my eyes and everything had stopped spinning.

> *"I declared I was healed and I was going to walk."*

I declared I was healed and I was going to walk. Feeling began to return to my legs! It seemed as if two million pins were pricking me because the nerves were being re-activated. I rejoiced because it was so wonderful to have feeling back in those lifeless legs...After a short time, the pain left....

Determined now more than ever to walk, I held onto the bedpost and cautiously took a step. Then I took another. Holding onto pieces of furniture, I managed to walk around the room one time.

I told no one of this, but the next morning I got up and did the same thing. That night I asked my mother to bring me some clothes because I was going to get up and go to the breakfast table the next morning. She was shocked, but she did as I asked. On the third morning I got out of bed, dressed myself, walked into the kitchen, and joined my family at the breakfast table. And I've been doing it ever since. [1]

Kenneth E. Hagin began pastoring at 17 and pastored for several years. Then the Lord called Him into a traveling ministy.

"Go teach My people faith!" the Lord said. "I have taught

you faith through My Word and through experience. Now go teach My people faith."

For years Brother Hagin traveled throughout the nation, teaching and ministering on faith and healing.

In 1963, the Lord directed Kenneth Hagin to move from Texas and to establish an office in Tulsa, Oklahoma. From Tulsa, in ever increasing ways, the Lord guided Kenneth Hagin in the teaching of His people.

An emphasis the Lord made was the putting of all his teachings into print. He told him that the printed page is the number one way to spread the Word.

A LIFE-CHANGING DAY

So, you can see what a crisis it was when just a short time after I started working at the ministry, someone had to be let go over just that, putting Kenneth Hagin's teachings into print. Actually, it was the *not-putting* of Kenneth Hagin's teachings into print.

One of the avenues the ministry used to obey the Lord in putting Brother Hagin's teachings into print was a four-page monthly magazine, *The Word of Faith.*

About the time they hired me, the ministry hired a man to edit Kenneth Hagin's teachings into print. It just so happened, however, the gentleman had some theological differences with Kenneth Hagin. They had been showing up, and one day it came to a head.

I remember the day so well. The office space was crowded. So I heard the reaction when the printer delivered the stacks of *The Word of Faith* for us to bundle and send out to the mailing list.

I remember that it looked good. About the only thing the budget allowed was the use of two colors of ink. The editor had chosen very light beige paper, dark brown ink, and orange for certain heads, etc. But there was a problem; it did not contain a teaching by Kenneth E. Hagin. The editor had chosen to use an article by someone else.

The decision was made that the gentleman would have to go, immediately.

"But what will we do?" Buddy Harrison asked Harvey Watson.

Harvey, whose expertise was accounting and consulting, came in every month from where he lived in the South, to look over our books and to advise on other matters.

He just happened to be there when *The Word of Faith* was delivered. It was Harvey who advised that the man be let go.

"Well," Harvey said, pointing to me, "we will let her do it until we can get someone else."

They never got anyone else.

The Lord placed me in the position that became my School of the Spirit for the next ten years.

---

1. Kenneth E. Hagin, *I Believe in Visions*, (Tulsa, OK: RHEMA Bible Church, Kenneth Hagin Ministries, 1984), pp 23-25.

CHAPTER 7

MY ANSWER: YOU CAN ANSWER THE CALL

My mother, Marie Combs, was a published writer. She'd had published magazine and newspaper articles, stories for children's books, and Sunday School material. (Years later, she was the first editor for Harrison House Publishing. She edited the early books of Charles Capps, Dr. Frederick K.C. Price, Reverend Charles Cowan, and others.) Writing was in my genes. I had studied English and had a paper published in college. So I knew I could do the job.

With a deadline approaching, I immediately began the wonderful job of putting Kenneth Hagin's lessons into print.

I moved to an upstairs office in the former bedroom of Buddy and Pat Harrison's daughters, Candace and Cookie. It was bright pink, with twin sinks at a bathroom-type counter along one wall.

Most of all, it was a quiet, somewhat secluded, place to work.

TRUTH: ANTIDOTE FOR ERROR

As he always does, the enemy attacked the move of God. Extreme submission teaching flooded Charismatic meetings and publications. And, as is often the case, one of the enemy's targets was women.

Women, according to this pervasive false teaching, could do almost nothing in the church. Not only could they not preach, they could make no decisions—certainly not in the church, and if they had a husband, not even in their homes.

Wives could in no wise have anything to do with spending the family's money without specific permission from their husbands. They could not balance bank accounts. Even if they were good with budgets and figures, and their husbands were not.

And according to one extreme teaching, when the gifts of the Spirit were moving in a service, wives were to move in close to their husbands for protection, for they were not capable to discern the spirits. They could read only the passages in the Bible that their husbands told them to read.

Now, if their husbands were unbelievers, all the rules still applied.

If their husbands went to bars and nightclubs, etc., they were to follow. If their husbands did not want the family to attend church, they were not to attend church. They were to stay at home with their husbands. They were in all cases to submit to their husbands without question.

Terrible things were happening in homes, and churches, as a result of such teachings.

The Lord directed Kenneth E. Hagin to conduct a seminar and to bring forth truth from the Word of God on the matter. It was entitled: *The Woman Question.*

It was my job to edit a book from the transcripts of the seminar.

How ironic that the first book I edited from Kenneth E. Hagin's teachings, was *The Woman Question.*

ANOTHER LIFE-CHANGING DAY

I remember that life-changing day very well.

As I sat at my typewriter in the pink bedroom turned office, typing the truths from God's Word as Brother Hagin elaborated on scripture after scripture, I began to cry.

The Word was making me free, just as Jesus promised it would.

"You shall know the truth, and the truth shall make you free...If the Son therefore shall make you free, you shall be free indeed" (John 8:32, 36).

I remember laying my right arm over the typewriter, resting my face upon it, and weeping.

> *The Word was making me free, just as Jesus promised it would.*

A Presence came into the room. I did not see anyone, but I sensed that someone from the realm of the spirit was in my office in a high degree of manifestation. I believe it was either the Lord, or an angel. A loving aura enveloped me.

I did not look up from where my head was over the typewriter.

Weeping, I asked aloud the question, "Do you mean I can answer the call to preach and not get in trouble at the judgment seat of Christ?"

Yes, you can, the Presence answered. *In fact one day you will leave here, and do just that. But right now, you don't know enough. And this is your Bible School.*

CHAPTER 8

SCHOOL OF THE SPIRIT

Right away, I saw that the practice of prayer in this ministry was different than what I had known. I found out about a prayer called "the prayer of faith." And I found out that there were other different kinds of prayers—only one of which needed the phrase, "If it be Thy will."

The denomination I grew up in prayed for the sick, all right. We did it in this manner. We put the names of the sick on a board and prayed that God would heal them. But we closed every prayer by saying, "If it be Thy will."

We were no more assured about each case after we prayed, than we were before we prayed. It might be His will to heal one. And it might not be His will to heal another. You just never knew.

IGNORANCE AND THE THIEF

Ignorance of God's Word had long hindered me from receiving answers to prayer. For instance, I remember clearly a specific time that it did.

We needed more money for our family of six. As the children grew, their needs grew. I decided to ask the Lord for

Kent's income to increase.

I prepared to approach the Lord. I chose a time when no one would be at home to interrupt. I dressed nicely. I cleaned our bedroom. I made up our bed with special care—there was not a wrinkle in the white bedspread. Then I knelt beside the bed, bowed my head, and began, "Dear Lord...."

I proceeded to set forth my cause with carefully designed words. We needed more money, I stressed, primarily for the children.

Out of nowhere, a foreign thought invaded my mind!

What about the starving children in India?

It was not audible. Yet I could hear it speaking in slowly enunciated, oh-so-religious, singsong tones. It made me feel selfish.

> *He could feed all the starving children on the planet, and it would not deplete Him one iota.*

So I stopped my petition, and said, "Oh, Lord. That's all right. You take care of the starving children in India. Kent and I will figure out something for our children."

As if God could be depleted! As if His supplying our four would somehow prevent Him from feeding four children on the other side of the world. He could feed all the starving children on the planet, and it would not deplete Him one iota.

Now I know it was the thief, coming to steal, who shot that pathetic thought across my mind (John 10:10). He not only did not want us to receive the immediate blessings we needed, he did not want me to know that I could pray and expect answers.

Now I see the foolishness of it. And I remember quite well when I first saw just why it was so foolish. I heard a minister teach something to this effect.

"God is not moved by need. It is the devil that creates need. If God were moved by need, He would be following the devil. The devil would be leading God; and that will never happen. The devil would be starting fires, and God would be running around after the devil putting them out. It is faith, not need, that receives from the kind, loving, giving hand of God. God has a wonderfully fair and safe plan, whereby His blessings are available to all through the avenue of faith; and He is not compromised into following after the creator of need."

THE HOLY SPIRIT - HELPER IN PRAYER

Back in 1967, early in the week of Kenneth Hagin's seminar, I picked up a book off the book table. It was a hot title at the time, John Sherrill's investigative book, *They Speak With Other Tongues.*[1]

A statement in that book intrigued me. Sherrill wrote that people who spoke with tongues claimed they could pray about things, even when they didn't know how to pray in their known languages.

I was so intrigued because of a tragedy—the sudden death of the 18-year-old daughter in a family who were close friends with my husband's family. Details were somewhat hush-hush. I sensed a great need for prayer, but I didn't know how or what to pray.

Later that week in the seminar, Kenneth E. Hagin expounded on the following scriptural basis for praying in tongues, when you don't know what to pray for as you ought.

> **ASV**
> **Rom. 8:26** And in like manner the Spirit also helpeth our infirmity: for we know not how to pray as we ought; but the Spirit himself maketh intercession for *us* with groanings which cannot be uttered;
> **Rom. 8:27** and he that searcheth the hearts knoweth what is the mind of the Spirit, because he maketh intercession for the saints according to *the will of* God.

Very soon after this lesson, I received the baptism with the Holy Spirit, and the accompanying evidence of speaking with other tongues. One of the first things I did was pray in tongues for that family. I prayed in such faith, for I had the Word on it. A strong anointing came upon me, and upon my prayers for this dear family.

The Spirit of the Lord was helping me pray, and I knew it!

A WORD OF KNOWLEDGE

But it was in 1970, not long after I went to work as editor at Kenneth Hagin Ministries that I accidentally discovered how "the gifts of the Spirit" also work in prayer.

To give you some background information, we had two huge typesetting machines called Justawriters, which we used to put out *The Word of Faith.* The big black monstrosities, now dinosaurs of the publishing world, were about the size of a refrigerator. Each machine produced only one size of type. One produced 12 point, and the other produced 8 point. The operator, me at the time, sat at the keyboard on the front, and typed the copy. It came out on white paper ready for paste-up. The copy was justified, aligned on both the left and right. These archaic machines saved us time and money. We could produce our own printouts, without sending copy outside to typesetters.

Our Justawriters were old, even then, and quite sensitive. The only company that serviced them was in Oklahoma City.

I had barely learned to use them when, with a deadline looming, one Justawriter produced badly broken type. A repairman could not come for days. Yet I did not think to pray about it.

After supper that evening, I got a phone call asking me to pray about a very sick baby. So I went into the parlor of our old home to pray. The parlor was the one room that was always neat. And I could close the French doors for privacy. I knelt beside the fancy old brown velvet sofa and prayed for the baby. Then I began to pray in the Spirit, in tongues.

After a very short time, I heard a Voice in my spirit. It was the authoritative Voice of the Holy Spirit. It was clear.

You have put the ribbon on upside down. Turn the ribbon over.

Justawriters, like typewriters, used ribbons. I couldn't wait to get to work the next morning. When I arrived, I ran right upstairs to the troubled Justawriter. I removed the ribbon and turned it over. It worked! The Holy Spirit was right!

The spiritual gift called "the Word of knowledge" gave me the answer to a very natural problem. (See 1 Cor. 12:8.)

God has all knowledge. Just as a word is a fragmentary part of a sentence, the gift of the word of knowledge is a fragmentary part of the knowledge of God.

I learned by experience that the nine gifts of the Holy Spirit work in prayer (1 Corinthians 12:7-11).

MY SCHOOL OF THE SPIRIT

And so it began, my school of the Spirit. From elementary levels, through intermediate steps, it continues to this day. Our subject in this book is prayer. Specifically *praying in the end of days.* So I will make an effort to confine herein, the lessons I've learned through many years, to those associated with prayer.

> *I learned by experience that the nine gifts of the Holy Spirit work in prayer.*

Everything I share later, in the "How-To" section of this book, began with those baby steps back at Kenneth Hagin Ministries. My schooling progressed, more and more, through the many generals in prayer that the Lord brought across my path.

And, very early on, the Lord made me to know that I had a heritage of prayer, even Holy Ghost praying-in-tongues prayer. It came to me through my father's family.

---

1. John Sherrill, *They Speak With Other Tongues,* (Minneapolis, MN: CHOSEN, a division of Baker Publishing Group).

CHAPTER 9

PENTECOSTAL BEGINNINGS

Growing up, I knew nothing of our family's Pentecostal roots—although I knew very well Great Grandmother Carrie Pickard, who was a major participant in those beginnings. Not long after I was baptized with the Holy Spirit, my father and his family began to tell me of our Pentecostal roots. And one memorable day, Daddy took me out to the old Pickard Place and showed me the canyon on Isaac and Carrie Pickard's farm where the area's early day Pentecostals prayed.

FROM MISSOURI TO OKLAHOMA

To my knowledge, the chain of events that led to the Pickard Place in Coweta, Oklahoma, began like this in the late 1800s in north-central Missouri near Fayette and Rocheport.

My great-great grandmother, Lou (Jackman) Pipes, a widow, with the help of her children, farmed the land she inherited from her father. Their big white Missouri farmhouse stood at the front of the farm near the road.

Life on the farm was hard work, but Lou ran an orderly, prosperous operation. Their rural surroundings were serene, quiet. Until—

Until a noisy family from Canada, with lots of sons, moved onto the farm across the road. The new Pickard family's loud music making and revelry was the talk of the countryside.

Things settled down, however, and the community grew to like the friendly Pickards. The Widow Pipes even married the oldest son, Levi. And eventually, her daughter, Carrie, married the youngest Pickard son, Isaac.

To Carrie's consternation, she learned one major factor in Ike's merrymaking was his love for the jug. So—when Ike excitedly suggested moving to what is now Oklahoma for land and opportunity, Carrie somewhat reluctantly agreed. She'd heard liquor was against the law in Indian Territory.

In 1901, Carrie and Ike, and their three little girls, set off in two covered wagons loaded with their belongings. After several grueling days on the road, they crossed the border into Indian Territory. To Carrie's dismay, the first person she saw was obviously drunk. Her hopes were dashed. And she had left her beloved mother and the countryside she loved.

Carrie and Ike journeyed on to the three-year-old community called Tulsey Town. They bought a farm at what later came to be South Peoria. But homesick and disillusioned, Carrie never liked the Tulsa area. After attending the burial of a neighbor's baby in the new cemetery at what is now 51st and Memorial, Carrie made up her mind.

How could that mother leave her baby in that forsaken wilderness? Ike could either take her back to Missouri, or he could move her to Coweta, where she could be near her Aunt Sallie Hurt. After all, according to Aunt Sallie, who ran a boarding house there, Coweta was the most promising town in the whole of the territories.

Ike realized how determined his young wife was. So they sold out and bought a farm in the sand hills, less than two miles south of Coweta.

THE NEW WINE

Cotton was king. The Pickards cleared their land and plant-ed cotton and other crops. It became Ike's custom, whenever he took a load of cotton to the gin, or went to town for other reasons, to get drunk before he headed home. The team of horses knew the way home from town out to the Pickard Place. Ike whooped and hollered and sang all the way. Carrie would hear him and open the gates.

> *But this time, he was drunk on the new wine!*

One evening, something aroused her attention. She listened more closely as the wagon drew nearer. Ike's singing was unusually boisterous.

"Girls," she said. "Go open the gate for Papa. He's drunker than ever!"

And he was!

But this time, he was drunk on the new wine!

CHAPTER 10

CHANGE AS THE CENTURY TURNS

Ike had come face to face with one of the breakthroughs from Heaven around the beginning of the prophetic 20th century. For at the turn of the century, in several realms important to God's plans and purposes, things began to change exponentially. They had to change. The end of *the end of days* was at hand.

We will get back to my great grandparents in the next chapter, but it is important to see what was happening in the earth.

Right around the turn of the century, parallel changes, divine in orchestration, occurred in the three people groups of Bible prophecy: the Jews, the Nations, and the Church (1 Corinthians 10:32).

In the scientific realm, for instance, in the almost 6000 years since the creation of man, technological progress was relatively slow. For most of those years, people traveled no faster than the legs of horses, or winds in the sails of ships, could carry them.

But God allowed such illumination on the subject of *light,* through men like Einstein, Edison, and others, that it brought us in a little over one century to the technology of today.

My Grandfather Coday (1891-1974) as a boy, endured the rigorous travel by covered wagon to Oklahoma. Yet he lived to sit in his comfortable living room, in front of his television set, and watch a man walk on the moon. That's phenomenal change in one man's lifetime.

In the realm of biblical prophecy, God brought great change in Israel—His prophetic time clock. After thousands of years, He stirred Jews across the Diaspora that it was time to come home to their Promised Land.

> *In the realm of biblical prophecy, God brought great change in Israel— His prophetic time clock.*

Simultaneously, God put it into the heart of widely scattered Jews in Europe and Africa. He stirred Theodore Herzl to rally European Jews to Zionism, and the establishment of a Zionist state. (Zionism is the belief that Jews are to return to Zion, the Promised Land.) At the same time, Jews in Yemen began to walk across the desert to that Promised Land.

This long ago prophesied *Ingathering of Israel* is the biggest sign of the coming of the Messiah, and the soon approaching visible kingdom of His Millennial reign. Therefore we know we are at the end of the sixth day. (See Chapter 14 in this book.)

In the Church, God restored what had been largely lost

of *the early rain* outpouring of the Holy Spirit on the Day of Pentecost (Acts Chapter Two).

The restoration began, in this hemisphere, with *a latter rain outpouring* of the Holy Spirit in Topeka, Kansas on January 1, 1901.

[At about the same time, a restoration of the Holy Spirit baptism came to Russia and Armenia. You can read the account of some of the very supernatural events in Demos Shakarian's book, *The Happiest People on Earth*.[1]]

PENTECOST COMES TO AMERICA

Reverend Charles Parham was led of the Lord to begin a Bible school in Topeka, Kansas. Someone told him of a large abandoned Tudor style mansion on the outskirts of town.

I'm going to quote what that great spiritual giant, John G. Lake, who received the baptism in the Holy Spirit in 1907, said about it:

> It contained twenty-two or more rooms and it was unoccupied. The owner lived in California.
>
> He went to see the building, and as he stood looking at it, the Spirit of the Lord said, *I will give you this building for your Bible School.*
>
> And he said to himself, "This is the house."
>
> As he stood there a gentleman came up to him and said, "What about the house?"
>
> Parham told him what the Lord had said to him, and the man being the owner of the house said, "If you want to use this building for a Bible School for God, it is yours." And he handed him the key without any more ado.
>
> The next day, he went to the train and met a young woman of his acquaintance. She told him that

when she was praying, the Spirit of God told her there was going to be a Bible School here, and that she should come. She was the first student. Thirty-five students came, all correspondingly directed by the Spirit of God.

This group began a study of the Word of God to discover what really constituted the Baptism of the Holy Ghost. After a month of study they became convinced that there was one peculiarity that accompanied the Baptism of the Holy Ghost—speaking in tongues.[2]

Dr. Parham was convinced that nothing tallied up to the Second Chapter of Acts, so the Bible school had a question, to which it actively sought an answer:

What did the Bible mean when it spoke of the baptism with the Holy Spirit?

In an article in the October 1906 issue of *The Apostolic Faith,* perhaps by its editor, William J. Seymour, this account was given:

> Just before the first of January 1901, the Bible School began to study the Word on the Baptism with the Holy Ghost to discover the Bible evidence....
>
> The students kept up a continual prayer in the praying tower. A company would go up and stay three hours, and then another company would go up and wait on God, praying that all the promises of the Word might be wrought out in their lives.
>
> On New Year's night, Miss Agnes N. Ozman...was convinced of the need of a personal Pentecost. A few minutes before midnight, she desired hands laid on her that she might receive the gift of the Holy Ghost. During prayer and invocation of hands, she was filled with the Holy Ghost and spake with other tongues as

the Spirit gave utterance.

This made all hungry. Scarcely eating or sleeping, the school with one accord waited on God. On the 3rd of January, 1901, Brother Parham being absent holding a meeting at the time, while they all waited on God to send the baptism of the Spirit, sudden-ly twelve students were filled with the Holy Ghost and began to speak with other tongues, and when Brother Parham returned and opened the door of the room where they were gathered, a wonderful sight met his eyes. The whole room was filled with a white sheen of light that could not be described, and twelve of the students were on their feet talking in different languages.[3]

SPREADING THE WORD AND THE SPIRIT

The Upper Room could not hold the 120 who drank of the Acts Chapter Two outpouring of the Holy Spirit. They spilled out into the streets of Jerusalem where Jews from three conti-nents, who'd come for the Feast of Pentecost, heard them speak-ing in their own tongues, "the wonderful works of God."

Just so, Topeka could not hold those drinking of the lat-ter rain outpouring. They soon carried their message, in pow-er and demonstration, to sur-rounding communities and states.

> *They soon carried their message, in power and demonstration, to surrounding communities and states.*

Dr. Pauline Parham was the wife of Charles Parham's only son, Robert. I am blessed to have known this great lady several years before she departed for Heaven. Her daughter, Bobbi Hromas, also a great lady, invited me to speak at graveside services for Pauline. I spoke at the concrete pulpit which marks Charles Parham's grave near Baxter Springs, Kansas.

I remember how Bobbi and I would ask Pauline why she hadn't kept a journal in those early days. She said that they were too busy to write. Once when Bobbi questioned her mother about telling some of their adventures, Pauline related this one.

She said that the Bible school students went out mornings into the community where they were holding meetings. They knocked on doors and invited people to come to the meeting that night.

They always wore white. Each day a few would stay behind to wash and iron the white clothes. Those staying in would also cook the noon meal. The team would come back to eat lunch, and then to rest in the afternoon before the night meetings.

One day when it was Pauline's turn to do laundry, there was a loud knock at the door. A distraught mother stood there with her dead daughter draped over her arms. I believe the daughter was about 12-years-old.

The mother said, "You advertise, Jesus Christ, the same, yesterday, today, and forever. Your signs on the tent say, the lame walk, the blind see, the dead raised. Well, here is my daughter. I want her raised before the authorities find out she's dead, and I have to turn her over to them."

Pauline invited her to sit down till the team arrived. The mother laid her daughter on the couch and sat beside her.

When the team came in, they gathered around the girl and prayed. She was raised up from the dead. The mother and daughter ate lunch with the team. They went to the meeting that night and gave testimony. Pauline said it was a powerful meeting! I would imagine so!

Bobbi Hromas, a highly accomplished woman, is director of American Christian Trust. She is married to Dr. Les Hromas, a world-renowned space scientist.

> *When the team came in, they gathered around the girl and prayed. She was raised up from the dead.*

Bobbi told me that for days after Miss Agnes Ozman received the baptism with the Holy Spirit, she could not speak English. She spoke only in an unknown to her tongue. The students attempted to communicate with her by writing. But she could only write in what to them was unknown tongues. When Charles Parham returned, he invited linguists to study the writing. It was Mandarin Chinese. She wrote, as well as spoke, for days in Mandarin Chinese. Bobbi still has those notes.

Eventually, Charles Parham and the early participants in the latter rain outpouring carried their message south to Houston, Texas where Parham started a Bible school.

A one-eyed black man, requested permission to attend.

William J. Seymour, son of former slaves, was allowed to sit in the doorway in those days of segregation. It was Brother Seymour that God anointed to carry the good news to Los Angeles where he became the leader of the Azusa Street outpouring. Segregation was unheard of there as the Spirit fell upon all who came. And come they did—from all over the world. The message and the outpouring spread to the four corners of the earth.

1. Demos Shakarian, as told to John and Elizabeth Sherrill, *The Happiest People on Earth,* (Fleming H. Revell, 1979).

2. John G. Lake, *John G. Lake, His Life, His Sermons, His Boldness of Faith,* Ft. Worth, TX: Kenneth Copeland Publications, 1994), pp 515, 516.

3. *The Azusa Street Papers,* [A Reprint of: *The Apostolic Faith Mission Publications* (1906-1908), William J. Seymour, Editor.] (Foley, AL: Harvest Publications), p 14.

CHAPTER 11

PENTECOSTAL ROOTS

Before Parham's group got to Houston, two women from Topeka came south with their message and its Spirit to the Tulsa area. Jeanne Wilkerson, well known Bible teacher and woman of prayer, told me about the two ladies. Quite a few people in Tulsa and surrounding towns, such as Coweta, Oneta, and Broken Arrow, received the message of a fresh Pentecost.

Ike Pickard crossed paths with some of the new Pentecostals on a Saturday, which started like many others. He'd sold a load of cotton, and was already "liquored up" when he passed the place where they were putting up a tabernacle. Much to the consternation of Coweta's civic officials and many of its citizens, the Pentecostals had secretly purchased property across the street from the largest denominational church in town.

Seeing the builders working outside, Ike stopped and asked if he could help. Ike, drunk or sober, was an especially friendly man.

They told him they needed lumber to build an altar bench. So Ike went with his wagon to fetch it. When he returned, he asked if he could be of more help.

"Yes. You can help us build it."

When the altar bench was finished, Ike asked, "Is there anything else I can do?"

"Yes. We need to carry it inside to dedicate it."

> *Ike was changed into a totally dedicated-for-the-rest-of-his-life, servant of the Lord.*

Inside the tabernacle, something more than the altar was dedicated. Ike was changed into a totally dedicated-for-the-rest-of-his-life, servant of the Lord.

Born again, and instantly sobered, he was filled to overflowing with the Holy Spirit, with the evidence of speaking and singing in other tongues.

Shouting and singing at the top of his voice, Ike headed home to give the good report to Carrie, the church-goer in the family. This was the singing she heard when she said, "Open the gate, girls. Papa is drunker than ever."

To Carrie, Isaac's account of what happened to him was not good news.

What is this heresy? she thought.

Coweta was troubled over the Pentecostals. When news of Ike Pickard's joining the Pentecostals reached them, the banker and some businessmen offered to help Carrie put Ike into a mental hospital.

Ike's transformation was amazing. But Carrie watched it through glasses colored by what the townspeople were saying about the holy-rollers.

Ike repeatedly asked Carrie to come to church with him. But she refused, until one Sunday morning when she was forced into it.

It was the Pickard's turn to board the schoolmarm, Miss Brooks.

When Ike asked Carrie that morning, Miss Brooks said, "Mrs. Pickard, anyone can see that something wonderful has happened to Mr. Pickard. If you don't go with him to church today, I am."

What a scandal that would have been!

Carrie and the children accompanied Papa to church. Once inside, Carrie could not deny the Presence of the same Spirit she was born of. Soon thereafter, Carrie received the fullness of the Holy Spirit, and joined her husband in what proved to be a lifetime of service to the Lord, especially in the area of prayer.

THE PRAYER CANYON

The Pickards became pillars in the Pentecostal community, right from its terribly persecuted start.

One night when they arrived at church, a dead chicken was fastened to the wooden stoop by an axe through its neck. A bloodstained note between the axe and the neck read: "If you cross this doorstep, next time this will be your neck."

That's why the praising, praying Pentecostals took refuge at the Pickard Place. A long deep canyon cut through the farm. In summer, they walked and prayed on the canyon floor. If they "had a burden" or "got happy" no critical ears could hear them. In winter, they prayed in the Pickard home.

Ike and Carrie Pickard became known as praying people, and the Pickard Place was known as a place of prayer.

THE PICKARD PLACE

Right after I was baptized in the Holy Spirit, my dad took me out to the Pickard Place. The old farmhouse was still there, but vacant. The land was used to raise cattle.

It was dramatic watching Daddy as memories rushed over him. At one point, overlooking the canyon, he fell to his knees and cried out to God. He asked the Lord to forgive him for those times in his youth when he made fun of the prayers walking the canyon. But I think it went deeper. I think he was asking forgiveness for walking away from his spiritual heritage. He immediately turned back to the truth of it, and he and Mom were soon filled with the Holy Spirit. The rest of their days, they walked in the fullness of the Spirit.

> *At one point, overlooking the canyon, he fell to his knees and cried out to God.*

Willie Combs, my dad, so loved his grandparents, Ike and Carrie Pickard.

Their youngest daughter, Nannie, married William Frederick Combs, the cotton gin owner's son. First, they had a daughter they lovingly called, "Little Jewel." Two years later, my dad, William Isaac Combs was born.

But one month's time brought tragedy, as well as bless-ing, to Nannie. On November 2, 1915, Little Jewel died from complications of chicken pox and pneumonia. My dad was born twelve days later, on November 14. Nannie was still in bed from the birth, when her husband died on December 3, 1915. A terrible accident, at the gin he ran for his father, caused his death.

Dad's mother was a wonderful woman. When I became aware of the difficult days she'd come through in the winter of 1915, I asked her, "How did you make it?"

She said, "I had to, because of him." And she looked over at my father, the one she always called "Little Willie."

Her Pentecostal parents took her and Little Willie into their home. Even after she remarried two years later, Nannie and her family remained close with Ike and Carrie Pickard.

My dad was a great storyteller, and he told great stories of life with the Pickards. He especially enjoyed talking to me about them, after I experienced the same personal Pentecost they knew.

As a very young child, he loved going with them to camp meetings. He told how they would go in a horse-drawn bug-gy, laden with fresh baked cakes, blackberry cobblers, fried chicken, Grandma Pickard's famous little biscuits, and coun-try butter and homemade blackberry or wild plum jelly for the biscuits. Yum!

One of their favorite places to go was Oneta, where some of the best camp meetings took place. It was less than a nine-mile trip, but Daddy said it seemed so far away.

Little Willie was as much at home sleeping on a pallet under a bench at his grandparents' feet, as if he were tucked in bed at home. For services went on into the wee hours of the morning. And they could last for days, or weeks.

Singers came from miles around. Lots of preachers, preached.

There was one preacher everyone waited for, Brother Billy _____. I don't remember the rest of his name. But he would get so caught up in the Spirit, that he would jump up on the altar bench. Then he would run from one end of it to the other, preaching and shouting, with his eyes closed. At some point, he would run right off the end of the altar bench. And there, in thin air, he would stop, and dance for a minute. Then he would run back onto the altar. The congregation waited for it to happen. And it often did.

> *There was always happy shouting, singing, and dancing in the Holy Ghost.*

Testimonies of divine healing and God's working in people's lives, punctuated the lively services. There was always happy shouting, singing, and dancing in the Holy Ghost.

My, How They Prayed!

What my dad talked about most, from the day he first took me to the Pickard Place in 1967, to the day he departed earth September 16, 2001, was how the Pickards prayed.

They believed they were baptized in the Holy Ghost and

given unknown tongues in order to pray about God's work. (1 Corinthians 14:2.)

Daddy said that at every meal, his Grandpa Pickard would say, "Pull out your chair, Son, and kneel beside it." In that manner, everyone at the table prayed.

Grandpa Ike Pickard's influence was indelibly imprinted on my father. Daddy prayed long, sincere, heaven-touched prayers before every meal.

Kylie, my oldest grandchild, laughingly says, "We never had a warm Thanksgiving, or Christmas dinner."

But we all loved every word, from the youngest child up to my precious mother, Marie Combs. We were blessed every time. At the end of his prayer, a few around the table could be seen wiping tears of blessing from their eyes. And after Daddy left earth, how we missed those long pre-meal prayers.

Isaac Pickard prayed all day long as he did the farm chores—loudly! After all, he sang loudly before he got saved.

My Aunt Lethy told me how she and her sister, Osie, were afraid of Ike Pickard when they were little girls. They had to walk along the dusty road past the Pickard place on their way to school. Ike would be milking in the barn near the road when the girls passed by. And, he would be praying or singing—loudly. Often in tongues! The little sisters always hugged the far side of the road and hurried past as fast as they could.

However, Aunt Lethy and her husband, Uncle Clarence Coday, became some of my best resources about the meetings in the area in the first part of the 20th century.

One incident they told me about several times. Two

young women were sitting together on a bench in the meeting. They were Aunt Lethy's mother, Mrs. Wheeler, and Uncle Clarence's mother, Mrs. W. F. Coday.

Several people saw something like a bolt of lightning, strike between the two women. One was thrown one way, and one the other. They both came up speaking in tongues for the first time.

Uncle Clarence and Aunt Lethy celebrated their 70th wedding anniversary before his departure. She lived past 100 years. Exactly to the day, one year before she departed, she had a visit to Heaven. She was told she must stay on earth another year, to pray.

Ripple Effect Prayers

The prayers of the first-generation Pentecostals were described to me in this manner.

As for location: They started with Coweta. Then they prayed out from there, geographically—that the will of God might be done in Oneta, Broken Arrow, Tulsa, all the state, all the nation, and around the world.

As for time: They started with the present. Then they prayed the will of God to be done until Jesus comes.

I believe the spiritual canopy of blessing over the greater Tulsa area, and the ministries and works of the Lord going out from there, was a direct result of the acceptance of the Holy Spirit outpouring by these early saints, and their faithfulness to pray.

After Grandma Pickard's death, they found an old prayer journal she'd kept in a small black book. I saw a notation which read: "Prayed for Brother Roberts' boy, Oral, today."

I believe that Dr. Bill and Vonette Bright's great ministry, *Campus Crusades,* without their being aware of it, and though the ministry did not develop until years later, may have been affected by such prayers.

Bill Bright's parents lived on the farm next to Will and Nannie Coday, when my dad was growing up. (Nannie Pickard Combs married William David Coday, when my dad was two years old.)

The Brights and the Codays enjoyed neighborliness, ice-cream socials, and the like. Glen Bright was my dad's best friend from boyhood. Little William (Dr. Bill Bright) was Glen's younger brother. When the Bright boys and Willie Combs headed out to swim in the farm pond, Little William would try to follow. Dad said they threw dirt clods at him to make him go back.

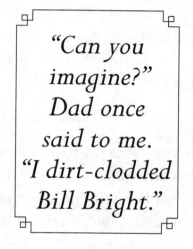

"Can you imagine?" Dad once said to me. "I dirt-clodded Bill Bright."

"Can you imagine?" Dad once said to me. "I dirt-clodded Bill Bright."

Right after the fall of Communism, I spoke in a minister's conference in Minsk, Belarus. We had a warehouse full of books to give away to ministers who'd traveled hundreds of miles across the former Soviet Union to receive the treasures. *Campus Crusades* had supplied thousands of Bibles. As I handed them out to the hungry ministers so thankful to receive them, my thoughts traveled back to Coweta, and the power of prayer. I wondered if the intricacies of this so-far-away-in-time-and-space cooperation between two ministries, whose family roots went back to Coweta, might have been prayed about by those saints praying "from Coweta around the world," and, "from now till Jesus comes."

Some years later, several people were standing in a hotel lobby in Washington D.C. after the National Prayer Breakfast. A powerful snowstorm had delayed our getting out. Next to me was Dr. Bill Bright. I told him about what happened in Minsk.

He smiled as he said, "Can anything good come out of Coweta?"

GRANDMA PICKARD'S PROPHECY

Isaac Pickard passed away when Daddy was thirteen; but Carrie did not move to Heaven until I was fifteen. I remember her well. She lived in a little house behind Grandma and Grandpa Coday. I spent many summers and every moment I could with my beloved grandparents.

She often drove her shiny black Terraplane coupe from Coweta to attend meetings in Broken Arrow where we lived. Evening services lasted late. When she crawled into bed beside me, where she always slept, I would rouse up. I was fascinated at how her body would *jump* a little as she exclaimed through the night, "**Hal**'lelujah! **Glo**'ry be to God!" Sometimes she seemed to spurt out in a strange language. I'd prop myself up on my elbow and look to see if her eyes were closed. They were. This happened in her sleep.

One Sunday is imprinted on my mind.

It was like almost every Sunday, at first. Daddy, Mother, my little sister, Pat, and I got out of church at noon. We drove ten miles to Coweta, where a delicious Sunday dinner awaited us at the Coday's house. My favorite was chicken and dumplings. Grandma started from scratch on Saturday by wringing the chicken's neck.

Usually, we had finished eating before Grandma Pickard got home from services at "The Old Mission."

That Sunday when she came into the kitchen to fill her little wooden ice bucket from Grandma Coday's refrigerator, our family was still around the table having the usual after-dinner discussion. Either politics or religion was generally the topic. That Sunday, it was religion. Daddy's family, and his sisters' families were denominational. The discussions were often about some of the tenets of faith of our denomination.

Grandma Pickard spoke up from the side of the room. This caught my 12-year-old attention. Usually she did not eat with us. And usually she was not there during the discussions.

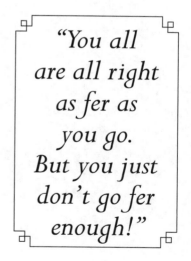

"You all are all right as fer as you go. But you just don't go fer enough!"

"You all are all right," she said, "as fer as you go.

"But you just don't go fer enough!"

Then she looked heavenward. Her face lit up. She shook her long bony finger and confidently declared,*"But one of these days, you're gonna see the light!"*

With that, she started laughing. Now I know, it was holy laughter. Then she danced right out of the house.

Not one person at the table said a word.

Her prophecy came to pass. The whole family came into the baptism with the Holy Spirit. I was the one with whom it began in that memorable April 1967 meeting in Tulsa.

CHAPTER 12

HELP THE PRAY-ERS

At the Lord's instruction, I resigned from Kenneth Hagin Ministries in July 1980. The time had come, just as the Voice said it would that day ten years earlier, when I was editing *The Woman Question.* Kenneth Hagin called me out in a meeting, and laid hands on me, ordaining me and separating me to full time ministry.

It was one year later, that I first heard the phrase: *Help the Pray-ers.*

In July 1981, I attended Hagin Ministries' week long Campmeeting at the Tulsa Civic Center. I arose early on Saturday to take a flight to Minneapolis where I was to speak in a campmeeting that night. When I got to my hotel room a little after noon, I was sleepy.

I remember saying aloud, "Lord, I'm going to take a nap. At 3 o'clock, I will wake up and prepare for tonight."

At exactly 3 o'clock, I sat straight up. I could still see the dream-vision I'd been having.

There was a great house. And in the great house there was going to be a great wedding. People were happily scurrying about getting ready for it. There was much excitement in the air. The Presence of the Groom could be sensed, but not seen.

I was excited too. But I was not scurrying about. I was sitting in an overstuffed armchair observing the festivities. One of my legs was propped over the chair's arm. In total comfort, I was drinking in the joyous scene.

To my left, and some distance away, there was a door. Someone opened it and called out to me, "Please help us get ready for the wedding."

> *"Please help us get ready for the wedding."*

"That's not my part," I called back, resenting the disturbance of my reverie.

I thought they were preparing food. I thought their part was to cook. I thought my part was to witness the ecstasy of it all.

A second time, someone called out from the doorway, "Come help us get ready."

"No," I said. "That's not my part. We're supposed to do our own parts. This is my part. That is your part."

The third time, the person literally cried, "*Please,* come help us get ready."

I did not go of my own volition. But I found myself transported into the room beyond the door. To my surprise, they were not cooking. They were unwrapping gifts.

At first, this irritated me. I told them, "You are not supposed to unwrap the gifts. That's the bride's part." But then, extreme curiosity overtook me. I had an overwhelming desire to see what the wedding gifts were.

Each package was as tall as a person. Each was wrapped, and tied with a huge bow at the top. The workers took hold of the ends of the ribbons of the bows, pulled them in a graceful move, and with a swish the wrappings fell away.

Every gift was an article of clothing. The workers took the garments from the boxes, placed them on hangers, and hung them on rows of racks. The colors of the garments were brown, green, yellow, orange, etc. Earth tones.

It was at that point that I awoke, but I continued to see and hear.

The Holy Spirit was my interpreter. This is what I heard.

The gifts are God's gifts to the Church.

You have never yet seen the operation of Christ's ministry gifts, or what you call the gifts of the Spirit, as they were designed to operate. (See Ephesians 4:8-13; 1 Corinthians 12:1-11.)

What you have seen of them has adorned the Church for her earth walk. But before Jesus comes, you shall see the fullness of the operation of these gifts as they were designed to function. This will adorn the Church to walk in Glory.

My attention was drawn to other packages, standing a little further away. They were the same size as those I'd seen, but they were much more beautifully wrapped. Their coverings glistened gloriously, and they were topped with gossamer golden bows. They stood awaiting an unwrapping. I knew these were garments of Glory.

The interpretation continued.

The people who came to the door and called you are the pray-ers. The gifts are in people; and they must be unwrapped.

*The pray-ers have a major part in their unwrapping. I want
you to help the pray-ers.*

GLORIOUS CONNECTIONS

The Lord gave me a revelation of Glory that was foundational
in my ministry. He taught me about His Glory, and the Glorious Church. You can read that revelation in my book, *The
Blood and the Glory.*[1]

During that time of revelation, the Lord impressed me:
*In the Glorious Church, I have set Glorious Connections. Some
are from the past. Some are in the time of your work upon the
earth. You are part of a body. But there are those with whom
you will work more closely, like the fingers on a hand. The
hand is not separated from the body. It is not cut off and float-
ing alone out in the air. It will still rub the foot, and scratch
the back. But the fingers on a hand work more closely with
each other.*

From the beginning, God connected me with people especially anointed in prayer. They were generals in His ranks
of prayer warriors. One after the other they came into my
life—people who prayed on a level, and in a realm I had never even imagined.

Kenneth E. Hagin – Much of what I've learned about
prayer, and have included in the "How-To" part of this book,
started with knowing this man of prayer.

Rachel Teafatiller – I met Rachel in Collinsville in 1972
where she had been sent on an assignment from God to birth
a church that, in the last days, would follow the Holy Spirit
and not man. Rachel spent most of her life in prayer, praying

for other people. I walked closely with her until she departed in 2008.

Jeanne (Mrs. D. B.) Wilkerson – During the Vietnam war, Jeanne and a small prayer group met every night. The Lord translated her into cells of servicemen held in the prison in Hanoi. Astute in her knowledge of the Word of God, she taught with an anointing, and she was surrounded by an aura, that lifted her hearers into a higher realm.

Wilford and Gertrude (Lake) Reidt – Kenneth E. Hagin walked into my office one day with these two treasures. Gertrude was the daughter of John G. Lake. Will was a student in Lake's Bible School. The precious couple had driven down from the Upper Pacific Northwest after they heard about Kenneth Hagin and his Bible School. They practiced a life of God's love in intercession. What stories they told me of Gertrude's father, and of their own adventures in God!

> *These Glorious Connections were for His purpose, and my call in the end of days:* **Help the Pray-ers.**

Elsie Ford. Lena Blackwood Cain, only sister of the original Blackwood Brothers Quartet. Reverend J. R. and Carmen Goodwin (Papa and Mama, to many). Doc and Jeri Horton. Clyde and Eufaula McGee. Carl and Grace Roos. And later others....

The Lord set me in close fellowship with these people of prayer. These Glorious Connections were for His purpose, and my call in the end of days: *Help the Pray-ers.*

PHILLIP HALVERSON

This Norwegian saint, who even looked the part, especially impacted my life.

Kenneth E. Hagin first met him during a meeting in Minneapolis. Phillip Halverson's experiences in prayer were so unusual that he went to his pastor about them. His pastor said, "I haven't had such experiences, but there is a man coming to do a meeting here who has. Ask Kenneth Hagin."

Brother Halverson described his unusual prayer life to Kenneth Hagin. He said, "For instance, right now I am praying about one piece of candy and one cookie."

Brother Hagin laughed, "Why those are the nicknames of my granddaughters, Candy and Cookie. They are the daughters of our daughter, Pat, and her husband, Buddy Harrison."

Only a few months later, Buddy Harrison was hired as a leader of youth and music at the church the Halversons attended. Brother Halverson had prepared the way in prayer.

I met Phil and Fern Halverson through Kenneth Hagin Ministries. Eventually, the Halversons bought a second home in Tulsa where they held prayer meetings, open only to Rhema students. When they were in Tulsa, the Halversons attended our church in Collinsville. We were very close.

But it was hard for me to pray with Brother Halverson. As he prayed out in the Spirit in tongues, the utterance was permeated with phrases in English. It was so interesting to listen. Later you might hear those same phrases in the news. For instance, he kept praying *Grenada*. Some weeks later our marines were there.

Supernatural happenings in prayer continually filled the Halverson's lives. You can read some of them in their book, *Unseen Forces Beyond this World*.[2]

You can also watch him pray, as the Halversons were part of our extraordinary gathering of praying saints in Los Angeles in 1983. We have CDs or DVDs of that historic meeting: *The Secrets of Intercession*.[3]

The meeting in L.A. came about because of what Kenneth E. Hagin had walked into my office and said to me, probably in 1980.

He told me that those seasoned pray-ers I fellowshipped with were going to start going home, to Heaven.

He said, "If you don't get out of them what they have, we are going to lose it for the next generations."

> *"If you don't get out of them what they have, we are going to lose it for the next generations."*

So Kent and I hosted the meeting in the L.A. Convention Center April 6-9, 1983. (Later we discovered our dates were the dates of prayer at Bonnie Brae St., and the outpouring there on April 9, 1906, which led to the Azusa Street outpouring.) It was the first large meeting we'd ever had. We had it specifically to get out of those pray-ers what they knew.

But Brother Hagin prophesied something else that day he told me they would soon go home.

He prophesied to me, "You are to write two books on prayer. One an elementary book on prayer, the other about secrets of prayer you learned from these people."

The book you are reading is the first I have written on prayer. I have written partner letters and published a book of them. But this is the first time I have sat down to write a book on prayer.

The praying saints did start going home. With the departure of each one, I knew a treasure I'd been entrusted to know, had left my presence.

PHILLIP HALVERSON'S EXHORTATION

But Brother Halverson's homegoing affected me most. He was so accessible. And I missed that very much. Then too, the circumstances of his departure were entwined with a departure in our family.

On May 30, 1985, my only sibling, my dear younger sister, Pat, departed earth, after a sudden and short illness. She was only 43. During the two months she was sick, Brother Halverson "carried" me in prayer, as I continued to fulfill ministerial obligations.

On Friday night before her memorial on Saturday, we were gathered at my parent's house. The phone rang. It was Brother Halverson for me. The phone's long cord allowed me to go into a closet and shut the door. There in privacy, I absorbed the Comfort of the Holy Spirit ministered to me through this praying saint.

He talked to me for an hour and forty-five minutes. He talked about his prayers during those two months. He said the Holy Spirit had "taken up" with him for a man named Don. Don was Pat's husband, but Brother Halverson had not known his name.

He told me the attack on her was an attack on me. He said Satan was trying to make me quit. He said that for a long time the unction of the Holy Spirit had been upon him powerfully to pray for me, that I would fulfill the ministry. He said that I did not realize how important it was to the Holy Spirit that I not quit.

Then he closed by saying in a very strong voice, *"Never forget that the number one call on your life is to help the pray-ers!"*

It was the last thing he ever said to me.

> *"Never forget that the number one call on your life is to help the pray-ers!"*

PHILLIP HALVERSON'S DEPARTURE

The next day, Saturday, we had Pat's memorial. Sunday morning I went to church with Don and their daughter Donna. That afternoon, I went home with Don and Donna and prayed with them to be baptized with the Holy Spirit. After they received, I drove from Pryor to Collinsville, about 40 miles, with a note of victory in my heart.

When I walked in the back door, the yellow phone on the kitchen wall was ringing. Kent handed it to me. The call was from behind the platform at Living Word Christian Center in Minneapolis. Phillip Halverson had just left his earthly body from their platform in the evening service.

Here is Fern's account:

> ...Pastor Mac Hammond spoke of the future of the church and the urgency to enlarge. He asked Phillip to come up and pray with him.
>
> What happened was quite unusual. Phillip almost jumped out of his seat and quickly walked up the steps to be with Pastor Mac. It was unusual because Phillip always took my arm and wanted me to be with him.
>
> I automatically rose up from my chair, and...followed him.
>
> Was there something he knew that no one else did? I think so.
>
> Pastor Mac prayed, and then with great unction, Phillip began to pray.
>
> Suddenly, Pastor Mac and Phillip went down under the power of the Spirit.
>
> Phillip landed face up, right at my knees. (I always knelt on the platform when Phillip prayed.)
>
> As I was praying in the Spirit and looking down on my husband's face, he opened his eyes and looked at me. Then he closed his eyes for the last time, but I did not know it at that moment.
>
> All efforts to revive Phillip proved fruitless. He slipped away while praying in the Spirit. How like him![4]

It took a while for the congregation to realize he was gone. When they called my home, I could hear the singing of high praises in the congregation.

Later, I thought of how orchestrated his homegoing was.

I had heard Phillip often pray, "Abundant entrance. Arrangements." When I asked him about it, he would say, "Oh, some faithful saint is going home; and the Lord is having me pray about it."

When Kenneth E. Hagin heard about Phillip's departure, he said, "What a way to go!"

As we listened to cassette recordings of Brother Halverson's ministry the three months before his departure, we saw that he knew he was going. There was a countdown in his prayers. *Three months. Three months. Home free.* And then. *Two months. Two months. Home free.* And finally. *One month. One month.*

The Saturday before he left, he asked the Hammonds out to eat. He spent most of the time talking to Lynne, a woman of prayer. Afterward she realized he was turning over some of his prayer assignments to her.

He named two people and said, "Never stop praying for them."

I was one of those two. I know the reason for his instructions to Lynne. It is that these are *the end of days,* and working with God in prayer is of utmost importance.

> *It is that these are the end of days, and working with God in prayer is of utmost importance.*

Fern gave me one of Phillip's Bibles with her handwritten note on the inside cover:

Dear Billye,

You and I now have Phillip's Bibles — How he prayed for you! How he respected your ministry! No other name crossed his lips in prayer more than BILLYE! — borne of the Holy Ghost!

Again, I know why my name crossed his lips so often. It was not so much for me personally, but because of *the Lord's call to help the pray-ers in the end of days.* It is prayer and the pray-ers that are so vitally essential to God's plans.

---

1. Dr. Billye Brim, *The Blood and the Glory,* (Tulsa, OK: Harrison House, 1995). Chapters 1, 4-7.

2.   Phillip & Fern Halverson, *Unseen Forces Beyond This World,* (Tulsa, OK: Harrison House, 2000).

3.   *The Secrets of Intercession, Los Angeles, CA, 1983,* (Branson, MO: Billye Brim Ministries).

4.   Phillip & Fern Halverson, *Unseen Forces Beyond This World,* (Tulsa, OK: Harrison House), pp 255, 256.

Chapter 13

Prayer Mountain in the Ozarks

Not long after my father took me to the Pickard Place, and I began to find out about my Pentecostal great grandparents, and their part in the earliest days of the restoration of the baptism in the Holy Spirit, in the 20th century, I began to hear this phrase in my spirit.

The cord of your inheritance.

I looked in the Bible and found something akin to the phraseology in Psalm 105:11. What I deduced from it was, that somehow the prayer ministry of the Pickards was the cord of my inheritance.

Frequently, I took my prayer partners (we called ourselves the Sparkies) out to the Pickard Place to pray. Those who prayed with me there were Brenda Baeza, Patsy Behrman (Cameneti), Lynne Hammond, and Lucy McKee. What glorious times we had.

Through the years, as I heard more and more, *help the pray-ers,* I began to contemplate having a place dedicated to prayer. And, I really thought that place should be the old Pickard Place. But the people who owned it adamantly refused to sell.

TRANSFORMED IN A TRANCE

Then supernatural confirmation came. The Lord made me to know it was He who put the desire for the place of prayer within me. But the site He had chosen was not the sand hills south of Coweta.

In February 1995, I attended, with thousands of others, Kenneth Hagin's Winter Bible Seminar. One night, as often happened when Brother Hagin ministered, the Holy Ghost took over.

You can still see the "wild" service on YouTube. You can see how the people praised, sang, shouted, laughed, danced, and fell under the power of the Spirit.

But you won't see me. I was there. I had a good seat with other ministers and guests behind the podium in what could have been the place for a choir.

The reason why you won't see me is because I was not standing. I was not seated. I was lying flat of my back on the floor between two rows of seats. My hands were held straight up perpendicular to my body. I don't know how long I was in this position. But a long time.

I was in what the Bible calls a trance. I was vaguely conscious of what was going on around me, but I saw and heard in another realm.

I heard: *Coweta is not the place now. Branson is the place.*

There on the floor, thoughts came to me.

The property in Coweta was to hold me to the call until the time.

Corrie ten Boom's prophecy of a great last day move of God.

Branson would be a catalyst. God would draw people to Branson from the north, the south, the east, and the west. (That has happened, and continues to happen.)

There is a place near Branson. Angels are holding the land.

There is to be a Prayer Mountain. A place where prayer would be the atmosphere.

PRIVATE PRAYER

I was made to know that people could come to the place for individual prayer, as they do in Korea. It was to be a secluded place where laborers could come for rest and refreshing. A place where people could separate to pray about the will of the Lord for their own lives.

> *There is to be a Prayer Mountain. A place where prayer would be the atmosphere.*

As I lay on the floor in the trance, I saw the interior of a simple log cabin. I saw an iron bedstead covered with a patchwork quilt. A rag rug lay on the plank floor beside the bed.

There were to be prayer cabins, particularly for individual prayer.

CORPORATE PRAYER

There were to be places for corporate prayer.

Seasoned pray-ers would lead in waiting before the Lord, and in praying Holy Spirit-guided prayers concerning *the end of days.*

Two purposes were to be the aim of the corporate prayers:

    1) To Pray in the Plans of God.

    2) To Stop the Strategies of the Enemy.

God's plans are to be prayed through from the realm of the unseen, to the realm of the seen. Satan's plans can be stopped.

Two kinds of prayer:

    1) Individual Prayer.

    2) Corporate Prayer.

Two purposes in prayer:

    1) To Pray in the Plans of God.

    2) To Stop the Strategies of the Enemy.

SHARING THE VISION

That night, after the vision, I shared it with some experienced ministers in the car as we drove away from Hagin's meeting. They confirmed it was the Lord. One minister turned to me and said, "When you find the land, we will give you $50,000 for the purchase."

The next day was to be our annual board meeting. So I prayed much that night that the Lord would put it into the hearts of the board members, if it were indeed His will. I prayed particularly about Pastor Lee Morgans, the Vice-President of our ministry, with whom I had worked at the time for 15 years or so. Every time I'd mentioned getting the Pickard Place, Pastor Lee did not get a witness to it.

In a euphoric meeting, the board members all had the same witness of the Spirit I had. Lee shared how the Lord had put such a place as I described in his heart years before.

CONTINUING EDUCATION

The Lord continued to talk to me about it.

Not very long after, the Lord said to me, *There didn't have to be an Oklahoma City.* This was in reference to the bombing of the Murrah Federal Building, April 19, 1995, just two months after the night of the trance.[1]

Today we know so much more about the enemy's evil strategies in his struggle for survival. How plain it is to see that God needs people who know how to work with Him in *the end of days.*

He showed me how Daniel saw in the Word—Jeremiah's prophecies—where Israel was in time. And what did Daniel do about it? He prayed!

He showed me how He had taken me to Israel, and the nations of prophecy, and had given me revelation about the times. He said this would be a place to share what I saw with others, and then to pray about it.

Paul saw God's plan for the church—to build it for a habitation of God through the Spirit. What did Paul do about it? He said, "For this cause I bow my knees unto the Father..." (Ephesians 2:20-22; 3:1, 14).

He showed me that He would raise up a people here, who could work with Him as the Bible School of Rees Howells worked in WWII. He said we were of a different time, and it would be in a different manner. But the prayers would be just as effective.

> "*As nations raise up an air force, I am raising up a prayer force.*"

Through the many years now, He has said other things to us.

For instance, *As nations raise up an air force, I am raising up a prayer force.*

THE PLACE

Right away, after the trance in February 1995, we began to look for the place, trusting God to lead us to it. We saw several places. Some quite developed, near beautiful Table Rock Lake. One I really liked.

One hot day in late June, a real estate man drove us 17 ½ miles east of Branson to a secluded place covered with virgin timber. It was near a game preserve, and the land sloped down to the shores of Bull Shoals Lake. My parents, 78 and 80, Pastor Lee and his wife, Jan, and I trudged through the heavy timber, and heavier undergrowth on a 47-acre site which two brothers had for sale. The place was cut through with a canyon, and wet season streams and waterfalls. And it was very wet that year.

The next day, I flew to Nashville, Tennessee to speak in Charles Cowan's Campmeeting. I took a nap that afternoon, and when I woke up, a word from the Lord came pouring out my spirit like a river. I wrote it down.

On June 27, 1995, I heard these words in my spirit, just as if I were listening to an inner Voice speaking them to me:

"Give me that mountain," old Caleb said.
"Give me that mountain, where the giants raised their
ugly heads.
"Give me that mountain, and let me see,
the Spirit of the Lord give it to me."

"Give me that mountain," rehearse, My child.
Repeat the phrase, in your own style.
"Give me that mountain where the waters flow,
 in a canyon,
  like my grandfather's son did know."

The canyon is yours, the mountain, too.
I've given you a mountain view.
A view of the big picture, under My hand;
A view of how things do really stand.

Gather My pray-ers unto Me.
And I will gather My people, to come and see.
  to take a look into heaven with you,
   to take a look and a very long view.

Don't be afraid.
Don't be afraid.
You went to Hebron this very year,
 in the midst of giants,
  you showed no fear.

Now take this mountain and come to Me.
Bring others with you, on bended knee.
It will be the easiest thing you ever did do.
I will honor your faith.
Take the step and follow through.
I'll bring the people, and all you need...

It's your witness mountain.
Now follow through.

For the mountain I have given you!!!

I brought those first pray-ers unto you.
(Halversons, Reidts, Rachel, Carl and Grace Roos, etc.)
I have others. You'll see.
They'll come two by two, then three by three.

Welcome them unto Me.
They come. They come.
You'll be ready, too. I'll see to it....

Raise up these pray-ers.
I will work with them.
Prepare the place under My Grace.

The quiet place.
The secluded place.
Receive it.
And believe it.

(My spirit seemed to already have picked up that the land I'd just seen was the right place, as the word began. But this is the point where I actually knew it.)

I took you to that Mountain Hebron.
How many have gone?
If I led you to that mountain so far away,
Could I not lead you to the mountain you saw just yesterday?
I could. And I did.
The price is fair. Do not dilly-dally.
I want you on that mountain, and the mountain clear
*   (money and trees to fell) this very year...*

This thing has been growing in your heart 20 years.
Don't be afraid.
This is not haste.

I have just saved you time.
You were faithful.
And I am more faithful to you.
Buy the land from the brothers two.
Daniel and James — My names.
Even the community will receive you.
Even the community will believe you.
Arise and do.

Take your family with you.
You need natural support.
I have kept your father alive to give witness.

Abide in Me.
Abide in Me.
Stay in My Presence.
For you will see,
Your footsteps are ordered.
You are where I've caused you to be.
Yield to the Spirit; Yield to Me.

We now have almost 300 acres. And the most amazing thing to me is something we never could have imagined that hot summer of 1995 when we were trudging through the brambles. And that is, from this secluded spot, we have weekly noon prayer meetings where thousands from around the world can pray together—either live by streaming, or with the archived meetings.

God has us prepared for effective praying in the end of days.

---

1. Dr. Billye Brim, *The Blood and the Glory,* (Tulsa, OK: Harrison House, 1995), Chapter 11, "Tokens: Answer to Terrorism," pp 71-74.

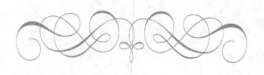

Section II

How To Pray

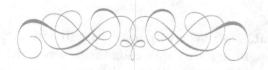

CHAPTER 14
THE END OF DAYS

What is meant by the phrase *The End of Days?*
First, it comes from the Bible. In the original Hebrew of the Scriptures it is: אחרית הימים *akh-ar-eeth' yom-im—The End of Days.*

Most English translations, however, translate the Hebrew words as, "the latter days."

The following scriptures are most of the places where the phrase is found. They provide insight into the term's usage and its time frame. I have quoted first the King James Version of each scripture, followed by a Hebrew translation of the same verse. I have started with the first mention of the phrase.

KJV
Num. 24:14 ...*come therefore,* and I will advertise thee what this people shall do to thy people in **the latter days.**

The Chumash, The Stone Edition, ArtScroll Series
BMidbar/Numbers 24:14
...Come, I shall advise you what this people will do to your people in **the end of days.**

KJV
Deut. 4:30 When thou art in tribulation, and all these things are come upon thee, *even* in t**he latter days,** if thou turn to the LORD thy God, and shalt be obedient unto his voice;

The Chumash, The Stone Edition, ArtScroll Series
Devarim/Deuteronomy 4:30
When you are in distress and all these things have befallen you, **at the end of days,** you will return unto HASHEM, your God, and hearken to His voice.

KJV
Jer. 48:47 Yet will I bring again the captivity of Moab in **the latter days,** saith the LORD. Thus far *is* the judgment of Moab.

ME'AM LO'EZ
Yirmeyahu 48:47 And in **the end of days,** I will return the captives of Moab, says the Lord; so much for the judgment of Moab.

> ME'AM LO'EZ Note:
> "...this, says the Daas Sofrim, is a tremendous promise; that long after the nation of Moab has been erased, and all but forgotten, it will be reconstituted once more and returned to its land.
> "...The end of days;" an expression always assumed to refer to the days of the Messiah."

Brim Note: Moab is in modern day Jordan.

KJV
Jer. 49:39 But it shall come to pass in **the latter days,** *that* I will bring again the captivity of Elam, saith the LORD.

ME'AM LO'EZ
Yirmeyahu 49:39 And in **the end of days,** I will restore the captives of Elam.

> Brim Note: Elam is Persia, modern day Iran.

KJV
Ezek. 38:8 After many days thou shalt be visited: in **the latter years** thou shalt come into the land *that is* brought back from the sword, *and is* gathered out of many people, against the mountains of Israel, which have been always waste: but it is brought forth out of the nations, and they shall dwell safely all of them.

Yechezkiel, The ArtScroll Tanach Series
Yechezkiel 38:8 From ancient times you are to be recalled. In **the end of years** you shall come to a land restored from the sword, gathered from many nations, upon the hills of Israel which had lain desolate continuously — and she had been liberated from the nations, all of them dwelling confidently.

> ArtScrolls Note: *Rashi*...You are to be recalled (that is, punished) for sins which were committed long ago...therefore — in order to facilitate your punishment — you will come in the end of years...

> Brim Note: Here the term is the end of years. אחרית השנים *akh-ar-eeth' h'shanim.* This substantiates the fact that the days are years. Just a few verses later (verse 16) the term is **the end of days.** Both speak of the same war.

KJV
Ezek. 38:16 And thou shalt come up against my people of Israel, as a cloud to cover the land; it shall be

in **the latter days,** and I will bring thee against my land, that the heathen may know me, when I shall be sanctified in thee, O Gog, before their eyes.

Yechezkiel, The ArtScroll Tanach Series
Yechezkiel 38:16...and you will advance against My people Israel like a cloud covering the earth. At **the end of days** it will happen, that I shall bring you to My land so that the nations shall know Me when I am sanctified through you before their eyes, Gog!

KJV
Dan. 2:28 But there is a God in heaven that revealeth secrets, and maketh known to the king Nebuchadnezzar what shall be in **the latter days.** Thy dream, and the visions of thy head upon thy bed, are these;

Daniel, The ArtScroll Tanach Series
Daniel 2:28 But there is a God in heaven Who reveals secrets and He has informed King Nebuchadnezzar what will be at **the end of days.** Your dream, and the visions in your mind, on your bed, are the following:

KJV
Dan. 10:14 Now I am come to make thee understand what shall befall thy people in **the latter days:** for yet the vision *is* for *many* days.

Daniel, The ArtScroll Tanach Series
Daniel 10:14 I have come to make you understand what shall befall your people in **the end of days,** for there is yet a vision for the days.

KJV
Hos. 3:5 Afterward shall the children of Israel return, and seek the LORD their God, and David their

king; and shall fear the LORD and his goodness in
the latter days.

**Trei Asar, The Twelve Prophets, Vol. 1
ArtScroll Tanach Series
Hoshea 3:5** Afterward the Children of Israel shall
return and they shall seek HASHEM their God and
David their king, and they shall tremble for HASHEM
and for His goodness in **the end of days.**

These Bible references shine light upon the Lord's meaning
of the times of *the end of days.*

A DAY IS AS A THOUSAND YEARS

Through two witnesses, one Moses and the other Peter, the
Word of God tells us that God sees time differently than we
do. With Him a thousand years of our time is as one day.

> **Psa. 90:4** For a **thousand years** in thy sight *are but* as
> yesterday when it is past, and *as* a watch in the night.

> **2 Pet. 3:8** But, beloved, be not ignorant of this one thing,
> that one day *is* with the Lord as a **thousand years,** and a
> **thousand years** as one day.

THE ORAL TRADITION

Judaism believes that God taught Moses an "Oral Torah." Moses taught it to Joshua. And Joshua taught it to others. And,
on and on, it was transmitted orally from generation to generation. It was not written down until the destruction of the
Second Temple, and the great diaspora (scattering) of the
Jews that followed. They decided it was necessary to commit
it to writing in the second century A.D.

One of the oldest traditions recorded is that God gave Adam a six-day work week to see what he could do with earth. The Lord worked in six days and He gave Adam six days. Each of Adam's days was to be of a thousand year duration. The pattern therefore is six work days followed by a seventh day, a Sabbath, of rest.

I first learned of this many years ago, studying the writings of Gordon Lindsay, noted biblical scholar, and founder of Christ for the Nations in Dallas, Texas. My studies since have found this to be widely accepted among teachers of Bible prophecy.

The following is printed verbatim as it is found in the Babylonian Talmud:

Babylonian Talmud: Tractate Sanhedrin
Folio 97a

The Tanna debe Eliyyahu teaches: The world is to exist six thousand years. In the first two thousand there was desolation; two thousand years the Torah flourished; and the next two thousand years is the Messianic era,

> Note: Messiah will come within that period.
> Note: He should have come at the beginning of the last two thousand years; the delay is due to our sins.

THE GRAPH OF DAYS

We have made the following graph to show the 6000 years since Adam's creation, and how the Oral Law divided the

6000 years into three parts. The third part, the last two thousand year period, is concurrent with "the end of days."

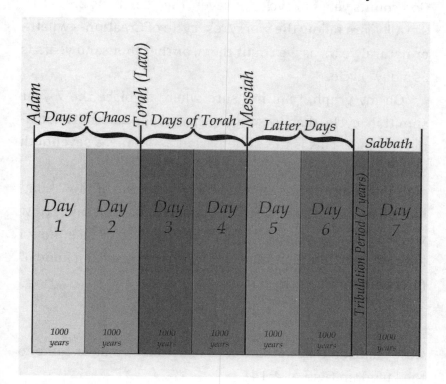

The Lord came right on time, at the end of the 4th day. The 5th and 6th days have been the days of the Messiah. We call them the Church Age.

When Peter preached on the day of Pentecost, the King James translates that he called it, "the last days." Having studied the scriptures in Hebrew, he probably said, "the end of days" (Acts 2:17).

When Peter spoke, it was the beginning of the period. We are now at the end of the period known as "the latter days," "the last days," or "the end of days."

SHMITTAH CYCLES

God counts years in cycles of seven. (See Leviticus 25:1-4.)

All years follow the work/rest cycle of Creation—whether natural years as we count them, or the "thousand years is as a day" cycle.

On my graph, I am not sure where to place the 7-year shmittah cycle that is sometimes known as "the tribulation period." This is the same period as "Daniel's seventieth week" (Daniel 9:24-27).

On this graph, it is shown at the beginning of the 7th day, but it may be at the end of the 6th day. For as Paul said, "Now we see through a glass darkly; but then face to face: now I know in part; but then shall I know even as also I am known" (1 Corinthians 13:12).

SELAH

How amazing that for such a time as this, we have come to the kingdom (Esther 4:14).

Whatever time period one lives in on the earth, one should know what God is doing during his or her lifetime. And then, cooperate with what He is doing.

If you lived during the time of Noah, you should have gotten your tools and helped him build the ark.

If you lived during the Master's earth walk, you should have baked some bread and cooked some fish, and gone to the meetings.

You and I live in a time that all the past ages have been moving toward. *The end of the end of days.*

We live at an age change!

Jeanne Wilkerson repeatedly said, "There are two golden hooks upon which all history hangs. The First Coming of the Lord! And the Second Coming of the Lord! All history pales in the light of these two events!"

You and I live just before the Second Coming of the Lord! The Bible calls our lives, our races.

Christianity is a great relay race. Starting with Peter and the Twelve, the Mary's, Paul, etc., on and on—the baton has been passed until it reached you and me. We are on the last lap of the race.

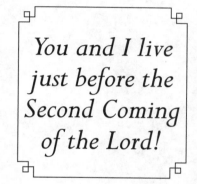

You and I live just before the Second Coming of the Lord!

The fastest runners are always put on the last lap of the race. It is our equipment—our knowledge of who we are in Christ, as revealed in the New Testament Letters—that enables us to finish in victory.

We are here to work with God, in His work just before the Second Coming, and all the great prophetic events associated with His Coming. One of the main ways He established for us to work with Him, is in prayer.

CHAPTER 15

KINDS OF PRAYER

An eye-opening, and guiding light on prayer, came to me from Kenneth E. Hagin's teaching on Ephesians 6:18.

> **Eph. 6:18** Praying always with all prayer and supplication in the Spirit, and watching thereunto with all perseverance and supplication for all saints;

Kenneth Hagin pointed out that "all prayer" in this scripture refers to the fact that there are different kinds of prayer.

Other translations confirm that fact.

The Amplified Bible translates, "all [manner of] prayer and entreaty..."

Moffatt's translates, "all manner of prayer..."

God's Word Translation reads, "Use every kind of prayer and request there is...."

There are different kinds of prayers. And the different kinds of prayers are governed by different rules.

Knowing this fact is fundamental to praying effectively.

Kenneth E. Hagin used the analogy of sports. There are different kinds of sports. And each one has its own rules of play. Playing one sport with another sport's rules would bring confusion. Imagine trying to play basketball with football rules. Imagine trying to play soccer with a tennis racket, and tennis rules. All these ball games come under the heading of sports; but in sports there are different games with different rules.

> *There are different kinds of prayer, and different rules cover them.*

Someone might ask, "Well isn't prayer, prayer?"

Yes. It is all prayer. But there are different kinds of prayer, and different rules cover them.

Someone once said to me, when I was editor of publications at Kenneth Hagin Ministries, "Brother Hagin is inconsistent in his teachings on prayer. He says that we can pray once, and believe we receive. And after that we can just thank God for the answer. But then in his book, *The Believer's Authority,* he says we can pray the two prayers in the Book of Ephesians every day."

This man was confused. He did not understand the teachings covered two different kinds of prayer.

In this chapter, I am listing some, not all, of the different kinds of prayer. These are basic. From the next chapter, I will major on prayer essentials for one who wants to work with God on *end of days* matters.

For further understanding of the basics of prayer, I recommend Kenneth E. Hagin's, *Bible Prayer Study Course.*[1]

THE PRAYER OF FAITH

Mark 11:24 Therefore I say unto you, What things soever ye desire, when ye pray, believe that ye receive *them*, and ye shall have *them*.

The prayer of faith is primarily about *you* and *your desires*. It applies to your situation and circumstances. This prayer is primarily effective in one's own sphere of authority. In other words, I can pray this prayer for myself, my spouse, my children in my house, and expect by faith to receive what God promises in His Word. I cannot pray this prayer for my next-door neighbor, and push off my will on him and his children.

And, of course, since "faith comes by hearing, and hearing by the Word of God," the prayer of faith is based on the Word of God.

When you pray, at that very moment, you can believe you receive, before you see any evidence in the natural, and you shall have what you believe.

The prayer of faith is governed by what John G. Lake called, "The inevitable law of faith." And that is, "According to your faith, be it unto you..." (Matthew 9:29).

Faith is governed by another law—the law of love. "Faith works by love..." (Galatians 5:6).

THE PRAYER OF CONSECRATION
VS
THE PRAYER OF FAITH

Because, this is such an important point, I have quoted extensively here from Kenneth E. Hagin's *Bible Prayer Study Course.*

> ...some people think you ought to end every prayer with the phrase, "If it be Thy will." When you question them...they'll say that Jesus prayed that way. But He didn't pray this way *every time* He prayed. He just prayed that way on one occasion and for one kind of prayer (Luke 22:42).
>
> For example, when Jesus raised Lazarus from the dead, Jesus didn't...say, "Lord, if it be Thy will, raise up Lazarus." No, Jesus said, *"...Father, I thank thee that thou hast heard me. And I knew that thou hearest me always..."* (John 11:41, 42).
>
> ...The prayer Jesus prayed [at Lazarus' tomb] was a prayer to change something. Anytime you are praying a prayer to get something, or to change something, never put an "if" in it. "If" is the badge of doubt. Should you pray that way, you're using the wrong rule, and your prayer won't work. It's that simple.
>
> What kind of prayer did Jesus pray, using the phrase, "If it be Thy will"? It was the prayer of consecration and dedication.
>
> There are other kinds of praying that will require the use of the word "if" when we don't know exactly what the will of God is in that situation...We use the phrase, "If it be Thy will" in our prayers because we want to be available to what Jesus wants us to do...to go anywhere, and do anything God has called us to do...Therefore in the prayer of dedication and consecration, we are to pray, "Lord, if it be Thy will," or "Lord, Thy will be done."
>
> However, when it comes to changing things and receiving something from God according to His Word, we do not pray, "If it be Thy will." We already know God's will because we have God's Word for it.

It is God's will that our needs be met. God wants to give us what we need. And we receive our needs met by faith.[2]

THE WORD OF GOD IS THE WILL OF GOD

Where the will of God is known, believed, and received, we can expect results.

> **1 John 5:14** And this is the confidence that we have in him, that, if we ask any thing according to his will, he heareth us:
> **1 John 5:15** And if we know that he hear us, whatsoever we ask, we know that we have the petitions that we desired of him.
>
> **John 15:7** If ye abide in me, and my words abide in you, ye shall ask what ye will, and it shall be done unto you.
> **John 15:8** Herein is my Father glorified, that ye bear much fruit; so shall ye be my disciples.

The fruit John 15:8 refers to is "prayer fruit." The Father is glorified in our bearing the fruit of answered prayer.

THE PRAYER OF COMMITMENT

A revelation I had to have in the area of prayer was regarding worry. For on one side of my family, they were champion worriers.

Where there is worry, there is no faith.

And, as Lake said, "The inevitable law of faith is, '*According to your*

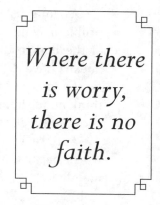

Where there is worry, there is no faith.

faith be it unto you'"(Matthew 9:29).

It's inevitable. You can't get around it. I can pray until I turn purple, and nothing will "be unto me," if I continue to worry and fret.

It was like water in the desert to the thirsty, when I heard Brother Hagin teach on how to pray *The Prayer of Commitment.*

> **KJV**
> **1 Pet. 5:7** Casting all your care upon him; for he careth for you.
>
> **Amplified**
> **1 Pet. 5:7** Casting the whole of your care [all your anxieties, all your worries, all your concerns, once and for all] on Him, for He cares for you affectionately *and* cares about you watchfully.

Brother Hagin shared about this in his book, *Prevailing Prayer to Peace:*[3]

> As long as you...fret and have anxiety concerning the thing you are praying about, you are nullifying the effects of your praying. You haven't cast it on the Lord; you still have it. If He has it, you don't have it.
>
> As long as you are still worrying about your problem, lying awake at night, tossing from one side of the bed to the other, trying to figure it out, He doesn't have it.
>
> As long as your stomach turns every time you think about it, as long as you can't eat for worrying about it, He doesn't have it. You do.
>
> And, really all of your praying about it will not work, because you have not done as He has commanded....

I pastored for about 12 years, and occasionally problems arose and I would be tempted to worry about them. When I would find myself becoming anxious about something, I would start talking to myself.

"Now Kenneth," I would say, "you know better than this. You are beginning to fret. Don't do it. It's not right."

Many times during the night I would awaken and the devil would bring to my mind a picture...I would be tempted to worry, but instead of worrying, I'd start laughing right out loud, and say, "I don't have that problem. I'm carefree. I don't have it, devil. You can show me a picture of it, if you want, but I don't have it. The Lord has it."

It is amazing what God can do with your problems when He has them.

It changed my life when I heard Brother Hagin explain a sort of "chess game" we can engage in with God. Its rules are in three verses.

KJV
Phil. 4:6 Be careful for nothing; but in every thing by prayer and supplication with thanksgiving let your requests be made known unto God.
Phil. 4:7 And the peace of God, which passeth all understanding, shall keep your hearts and minds through Christ Jesus.
Phil. 4:8 Finally, brethren, whatsoever things are true, whatsoever things *are* honest, whatsoever things *are* just, whatsoever things *are* pure, whatsoever things *are* lovely, whatsoever things *are* of good report; if *there be* any virtue, and if *there be* any praise, think on these things.

Amplified
Phil. 4:6 Do not fret *or* have any anxiety about anything, but in every circumstance *and* in everything, by prayer

and petition (definite requests), with thanksgiving, continue to make your wants known to God.

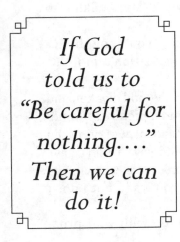

> *If God told us to "Be careful for nothing...." Then we can do it!*

First, it relieved my heart immensely when Kenneth Hagin pointed out that God would not ask us to do something we can't do. It would be unfair. If God told us to *"Be careful for nothing...."* Then we can do it!

I have written the Amplified translation of verse 6, in the margin of my King James Bible. It is so wonderful, *"Do not fret, or have any anxiety about anything...."* That covers it all, everything. And I can do it!

Kenneth Hagin taught something about these verses that I have made use of from the first day I heard it until today. He taught us that *doing* Philippians 4:6-8 is like engaging in chess, or checkers, with God. Some verses are our move. One verse is God's move.

He said, "God will never move out of turn. But He will never fail to move, when it is His turn."

Let me illustrate. And I have combined the King James Version and the Amplified.

> <u>Verse 6 is our move:</u> "Do not fret or have any anxiety about anything. But in everything by prayer and supplication with thanksgiving, let your requests be made known to God."

Verse 7 is God's move: "And the peace of God, which pass-
es all understanding, shall keep your hearts and minds
through Christ Jesus."

Verse 8 is our move again: Finally, brethren, whatsoever things are true...honest...just...pure...lovely...of good
report; if there be any virtue, and if any praise, think on
these things.

The first move is our move. We must do verse 6. God cannot
make His move and give us verse 7, unless and until, we have
done verse 6.

Next it is God's move. God will not fail to move when it is
His move. God will give us what verse 7 promises.

Then it is our move again. To keep what God gave us
in His move, verse 7, we have to do verse 8. We have to do
something with our minds.

OTHER KINDS OF PRAYER

The Prayer of Agreement — Matthew 18:19.

The Prayer of Praise and Worship — Acts 13:2;
Acts 13; 26, The Psalms, etc.

United Prayer — Acts 4:24.

These kinds of prayer are basic. We will move on now to
prayer of utmost importance for working with God *in the end
of days,* and indeed for life itself *in the end of days.*

1. Kenneth E. Hagin, *Bible Prayer Study Course,* (Tulsa, OK: Rhema Bible Church).

2. Ibid., p 45.

3. Ibid., *Prevailing Prayer to Peace,* pp 47, 59-60.

Chapter 16

A Body Prepared

Now we go a little deeper. Now we get more specific to *the end of days.*

The next chapter, "The Authority of the Believer," is of number one importance. In fact, I debated about whether to put this chapter first, or the next one.

Prepared for Him

One morning recently, just as I awoke, this phrase was going over and over in my spirit. *A body hast thou prepared for me. A body hast thou prepared for me.*

It was made known to me that another layer of illumination, of the meaning of the scripture, was being given to me.

Of course, in its basic meaning, the scripture speaks of The Messiah, The Anointed One. But on this morning, as I awoke, the Lord was revealing to me that the Church, the *ecclesia,* is prepared, and is being further prepared for Him.

One of the Lord's chief needs in the earth is a body through which to work. A body through which He can:

1. Bring His will—His plans—into the earth.
2. Stop the strategies of the enemy.

I knew that the words going round and round within my spirit were the words of the Anointed One, when He came from the regions of Eternity to walk in Time. The Words He uttered when He came to the earth to consummate the Father's Great Plan of Redemption.

> **Heb. 10:4** For *it is* not possible that the blood of bulls and of goats should take away sins.
> **Heb. 10:5** Wherefore when he cometh into the world, he saith, Sacrifice and offering thou wouldest not, but a body hast thou prepared me:
> **Heb. 10:6** In burnt offerings and *sacrifices* for sin thou hast had no pleasure.
> **Heb. 10:7** Then said I, Lo, I come (in the volume of the book it is written of me,) to do thy will, O God.

Just as Hebrews 10:7 declares, it is written in the volume of the Book of Psalms.

> **Psa. 40:6** Sacrifice and offering thou didst not desire; mine ears hast thou opened: burnt offering and sin offering hast thou not required.
> **Psa. 40:7** Then said I, Lo, I come: in the volume of the book *it is* written of me,
> **Psa. 40:8** I delight to do thy will, O my God: yea, thy law *is* within my heart.

God designed man for redemption.

God made man a creature of blood. God was not restricted to create creatures of blood. Angels have no blood. Lucifer was not created with blood.

God called man *Adam,* connecting him in the wonderfully revealing Hebrew language to blood (*dam*) and the ground (*adamah*). Both blood and ground are red (*adom*).

God put spirit-man, and his soul, into a body of flesh, made of the dust of the ground. (See 1 Thessalonians 5:23.)

Man's body—an earthen vessel—could be broken, and the blood poured out, a life for a life.

If a Divine One would go to earth, Incarnate, and live without sin in "a body prepared," His vessel could be broken and His perfect Life poured out in His Blood for the remission of all sin.

In some eternal moment, in some heavenly place, the One we call Savior agreed to consummate the Father's Great Plan of Redemption. First in Heaven, and eventually at Calvary, our Lord Jesus offered Himself through the Eternal Spirit, without spot to God.

Heb. 9:14 How much more shall the blood of Christ, who through the eternal Spirit offered himself without spot to God, purge your conscience from dead works to serve the living God?

In what is a great mystery, God the Son became, "...the Lamb slain from the foundation of the world" (Revelation 13:8).

Jesus came to do God's will. He delighted to do God's will. Every day of His earth walk, He did only God's will.

What a contrast to Lucifer.

Lucifer was the first one to cross God's will. He fell declaring five infamous "I wills."

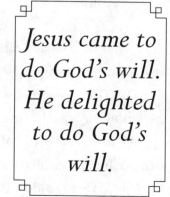

Jesus came to do God's will. He delighted to do God's will.

> **Is. 14:12** How art thou fallen from heaven, O Lucifer, son of the morning! *how* art thou cut down to the ground, which didst weaken the nations!
> **Is. 14:13** For thou hast said in thine heart, I will ascend into heaven, I will exalt my throne above the stars of God: I will sit also upon the mount of the congregation, in the sides of the north:
> **Is. 14:14** I will ascend above the heights of the clouds; I will be like the most High.
> **Is. 14:15** Yet thou shalt be brought down to hell, to the sides of the pit.

WE ARE A BODY PREPARED
TO DO GOD'S WILL IN THE EARTH

God has a will for the earth and its peoples. In our dispensation, we are to be His body, His channel through which He can get His will into the earth.

Christ, the Anointed One, is the Head; we are the Body.

> **Eph. 1:22** And hath put all *things* under his feet, and gave him *to be* the head over all *things* to the church,
> **Eph. 1:23** Which is his body, the fulness of him that filleth all in all.

"The church which is His body...." That settles it. The Church is His body.

The Greek word translated church is *ecclesia.* It means *assembly,* or a gathering of called-out ones.

We are a body of called-out ones from every tongue, nation, tribe, *assembled into a body* of which He is the Head.

John Wesley said, "It seems God is limited by our prayer life—that He can do nothing for humanity unless someone asks Him."

Why? It has to do with authority on the earth.

God needs a body through which to work on the earth.

A man I saw recently was wearing a T-shirt which said, "God doesn't need me. I need God." Sounds so religious, so humble. But it is untrue.

God needs a body through which to get His will into the earth.

> *It has to do with authority on the earth.*

Many scriptures attest to the fact that the *ecclesia* is that body.

We are a body prepared, and being prepared, for Him.

And He has given to those who are called believer's *Authority!*

The Authority of the Believer!

CHAPTER 17

AUTHORITY OF THE BELIEVER

Through my years at Hagin Ministries, I kept track of how many copies of each book title was published. By far, *The Believer's Authority,* outsold every other book.

In 1980, through very supernatural happenings, I began to go to Soviet Russia with Rhema Bible Training Center graduate, Jim Kaseman and his wife, Kathleen. We continued regular travel there to minister to the underground church through the days of Communism and even after its fall. Our amazing adventures are the stuff of another book I have long intended to write.

What is relevant here, happened because of the Lord's direction to Jim to get 3.3 million copies of Kenneth E. Hagin's books behind the Iron Curtain. I am witness to the fact that the Kasemans got the job done—3.3 million books printed and distributed, in KGB days! Accomplishing that feat, from translation, to delivery through every carrier imaginable, is worthy of inclusion in the Book of Acts, if it is still being written in Heaven.

One of those books, and the most important, was *The Believer's Authority.*

After Communism fell, Jim was watching a Network Newscast in which a high ranking Communist Chinese military officer was being interviewed.

The newsman asked him, "What was the cause of the fall of Communism in Russia, as you see it?"

He answered, "I know what happened in Russia. It was the Christians. And it is not going to happen in China."

East German Christians, testified at a Kenneth Hagin meeting in Broken Arrow, how they had received a German translation of *The Believer's Authority*. They told how they banded together and used the truths they learned to believe for a bloodless fall of The Berlin Wall. We received this testimony just after the fall of that wall, which was really the fall of Communism.

They humbly operate in authoritative power.

Understanding the authority of the believer, is of top importance in working with God in prayer *in the end of days.* For one thing, believers who understand it are not afraid. They humbly operate in authoritative power.

KENNETH HAGIN'S FOREWORD

Kenneth E. Hagin wrote the following in the Foreword to his book, *The Believer's Authority.*[1]

> Back in the 1940s, I asked myself the question, "Do we have authority that we don't know about — that we haven't discovered — that we're not using?"

I had had little glimpses of spiritual authority once in a while. Like others, I had stumbled upon it and had exercised it without knowing what I was doing. I wondered, "Is the Spirit of God trying to show me something?" so I began to study along this line, think along this line, feed along this line — and I began to see more and more light.

An article in *The Pentecostal Evangel* prompted my study on the words "power" and "authority." Then I came across a wonderful pamphlet entitled *The Authority of the Believer* by John A. MacMillan, a missionary to China [and the Philippines] who later edited *The Alliance Weekly...*

As a result of my studies, I concluded that we as a Church have authority on the earth that we've never yet realized — authority that we're not using.

A few of us have barely gotten to the edge of that authority, but before Jesus comes again, there's going to be a whole company of believers who will rise up with the authority that is theirs. They will know what is theirs, and they will do the work that God intended they should do.

In the last paragraph of his Foreword, Kenneth Hagin, I believe, prophesied the time in which we live—*the end of the end of days.* I believe we are that company, a prayer force, that is rising up with the authority that is ours.

JOHN A. MACMILLAN'S PREFACE

John A. MacMillan's pamphlets were put into a book that I preach from, and sell everywhere I go: *The Authority of the Believer.*[2]

People often skip *Forewords* and *Prefaces* to books, but this one is of immeasurable importance. When I teach on this subject, and that is often, I start by reading MacMillan's Preface. The italicized emphasis is mine.

> The rapidly approaching end of the age is witnessing a tremendous increase in the activity of the powers of darkness...[He lists several reasons for this that he saw.]
>
> To meet the situation the Church of Christ needs *a new conception of prayer.* The urgent call is for men and women, wholly yielded to the Lord, whose eyes have been enlightened to see *the ministry in the heavenlies* to which they have been called.
>
> Such believers...may in union with the great Head of the Body, exercise an *authority to which the powers of the air **must** give place wherever challenged.*

MacMillan departed earth in 1956. How much greater now is the increase of the activity of the powers of darkness. And how many more reasons for that rise do we see than he saw. Yet the powerful revelation in his book is the same revelation that will work for us today. And, like Kenneth Hagin prophesied, knowledge of this revelation is much more widespread among believers who will work with God in His eternal purposes.

TWO GREEK WORDS

First, the King James Version uses one English word, *power,* to translate several different Greek words. The two of most interest to us here are: *dunamis* and *exousia.*

The Companion Bible,[3] Appendix 172, defines their meanings under the heading "The Synonymous Words for 'Power'":

1. **dunamis** = inherent power; the power of reproducing itself: from which we have Eng. dynamics, dynamo, etc. See Acts 1:8.

5. **exousia** = authority, or, delegated power; the liberty and right to put forth power. See John 1:12.

A police officer does not have the *dunamis* to stop heavy traffic. Human physical strength is no match for a motor vehicle. But when a uniformed officer holds up his or her hand, all traffic stops. The authority, *exousia,* behind the badge demands compliance.

One scripture in which the KJV uses *power* to translate both words is Luke 10:19. I have inserted the Greek words.

> **Luke 10:19** Behold, I give unto you **power** [*exousia*] to tread on serpents and scorpions, and over all the **power** [*dunamis*] of the enemy: and nothing shall by any means hurt you.

The seventy, to whom Jesus spoke directly, did not have the *dunamis* power to dominate the demons of the kingdom of darkness. But Jesus delegated to them the authority to dominate Satan's cohorts.

Authority is delegated power.

Authority is delegated power.

Jesus defeated Satan and the kingdom of darkness for mankind by living a sinless life in the flesh... By His suffering and death at Calvary... By His triumph over death, hell, and the grave... In His making an open show of Satan's defeat...

And in His Resurrection. After He presented His blood to the Father, and the Father's acceptance of that blood, Jesus returned to earth, and said something to His disciples that applies to all believers thereafter.

> **Matt. 28:18** And Jesus came and spake unto them, saying, All **power** [*exousia*] is given unto me in heaven and in earth.
> **Matt. 28:19** Go ye therefore, and teach all nations, baptizing them in the name of the Father, and of the Son, and of the Holy Ghost:
> **Matt. 28:20** Teaching them to observe all things whatsoever I have commanded you: and, lo, I am with you alway, *even* unto the end of the world. Amen.

> *Authority is as strong as the power behind it.*

In His Great Commission, He said, *"All authority is given unto me in heaven and in earth, Go ye therefore..."*

Jesus delegated the authority on the earth to His body on the earth.

THE GREATER ONE WITHIN

Authority is as strong as the power behind it. The authority of the traffic policeman is as strong as the civic government behind him.

The power behind the body of Christ is the greatest power in all Creation—the power of God. That's why the Word of God declares, *"Greater is He that is in you, than he that is in the world"* (1 John 4:4).

1 John 4:1 Beloved, believe not every spirit, but try the spirits whether they are of God: because many false prophets are gone out into the world.
1 John 4:2 Hereby know ye the Spirit of God: Every spirit that confesseth that Jesus Christ is come in the flesh is of God:
1 John 4:3 And every spirit that confesseth not that Jesus Christ is come in the flesh is not of God: and this is that *spirit* of antichrist, whereof ye have heard that it should come; and even now already is it in the world.
1 John 4:4 Ye are of God, little children, **and have overcome them: because greater is he that is in you, than he that is in the world.**

Who are the "them" that verse 4 says we have overcome? They are the evil spirits written about in verses 1-3.

We have overcome them. Why? Because the Greater One lives in us!

We have authority over the kingdom of darkness.

We can, and we must, use our authority in *the end of days.*

---

1. Kenneth E. Hagin, *The Believer's Authority,* (Tulsa, OK: Rhema Bible Church, Kenneth Hagin Ministries), Foreword.

2. John A. MacMillan, *The Authority of the Believer,* (Camp Hill, PA: Wing Spread Publishers), p xiii.

3. *The Companion Bible,* (Grand Rapids, MI: Kregal Publications), Appendix 172.

CHAPTER 18

OUR MINISTRY IN THE HEAVENLIES

Christians have the authority to keep their areas free from shooting sprees at local schools, churches, malls, or public events. Christians have the authority to keep their areas free from epidemics of suicide. Christians have the authority to keep Satan from having high carnival in their homes and families.

Wherever demon forces are the culprits, we have the authority to keep them at bay.

The authority comes with the new birth.

But believers must know about it. And they must know how to operate in it. It is operated from a seat of authority at the right hand of the Father on high. A seat every believer can rule from, because they are seated there in Christ.

THE BOOK OF EPHESIANS

The principles of the authority of the believer are set forth in this New Covenant Letter to the body of Christ.

All the Bible is for the church, but not all the Bible is about the church. The part of the Bible that is particularly about the church is in the New Testament Epistles. The Epistles tell you who you are, what you are, and what you have, because you are "In Him."

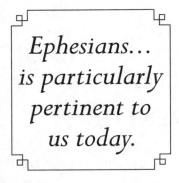

Ephesians... is particularly pertinent to us today.

Ephesians, even among all the Epistles, is particularly pertinent to us today. You should read the first two chapters right now.

Kenneth Hagin encouraged believers to pray the prayers in those chapters for themselves every day. They are Spirit given and anointed prayers that we may pray for ourselves or other believers. I have personalized those prayers and prayed them almost every day for many years. The "spirit of revelation" that has come to me, has come as a result.

THE FIRST PRAYER

Eph. 1:17 That the God of our Lord Jesus Christ, the Father of glory, may give unto you [unto me] the spirit of wisdom and revelation in the knowledge of him:
Eph. 1:18 The eyes of your [my] understanding being enlightened; that ye [I] may know what is the hope of his calling, and what the riches of the glory of his inheritance in the saints,
Eph. 1:19 And what *is* the exceeding greatness of his power to us-ward who believe, according to the working of his mighty power,
Eph. 1:20 Which he wrought in Christ, when he raised him from the dead, and set *him* at his own right hand in the heavenly *places,*
Eph. 1:21 Far above all principality, and power, and might, and dominion, and every name that is named, not only in this world, but also in that which is to come:
Eph. 1:22 And hath put all *things* under his feet, and gave

him *to be* the head over all *things* to the church,
Eph. 1:23 Which is his body, the fulness of him that filleth
all in all.
Eph. 2:1 And you[I, or we] *hath he quickened,* who were
dead in trespasses and sins; ...
Eph. 2:4 But God, who is rich in mercy, for his great love
wherewith he loved us,
Eph. 2:5 Even when we were dead in sins, hath quickened
us together with Christ, (by grace ye are saved;)
Eph. 2:6 And hath raised *us* up together, and made *us* sit
together in heavenly *places* in Christ Jesus:

This prayer is that we may have revelation in Him of three
particular things. They all have to do with glory, and the glorious church, but we won't go into that here.

1. The hope of His calling.

2. The riches of the glory of His inheritance
in the saints.

3. The exceeding greatness of His power
(*dunamis*) toward usward who believe.

It is only number 3 that we will go into here.

QUOTING FROM MACMILLAN'S BOOK
THE AUTHORITY OF THE BELIEVER

MacMillan's book is so outstanding that for the rest of this
chapter, I am quoting from it. I am not using the smaller type,
because I want you to read it. The following, to the end of this
chapter, is quoted verbatim, just in case:

*The Authority of the Believer, John A. MacMillan,
Portions of Pages 5-23*
When the Lord Jesus, the Captain of our salvation, was raised

from the dead, the act of resurrection was accomplished through "the exceeding greatness of His [God's] power [*dunamis*], to usward who believe, according to the working [*energeian*] of the strength [*kratous*] of His might [*ischuous*]."

In this working there was such a putting forth of the divine omnipotence that the Holy Spirit, through the apostle, requires four [Greek] words to bring out the thought...their combination signifies that behind the fact of the resurrection of the Lord Jesus there lay the mightiest working recorded in the Word of God.

Having been thus raised from among the dead, Christ Jesus was exalted by God to His own right hand in the heavenlies...

The resurrection had been opposed by the tremendous "*powers of the air:*" "all principality, and power, and might, and dominion, and every name that is named, not only in this world [*aion,* age] but also in that which is to come" (Ephesians 1:21).

The evil forces of the "age to come" had been arrayed against the purpose of God. They had, however, been baffled and overthrown, and the risen Lord had been enthroned "far above" them, ruling with the authority of the Most High.

To Usward Who Believe

All the demonstration of the glory of God, shown in the manifestation of His omnipotence, pointed manward. The cross of Christ, with what it revealed...shows us a representative Man overcoming for mankind and preparing, through His own incumbency, a throne and a *heavenly ministry* for those who should overcome through Him...

...Christ and His people were raised together.

...the reviving of Christ expresses also the reviving of His people. That is to say the very act of God which raised the Lord from among the dead, raised also His body. Head and body are naturally raised together: Christ, the Head; His body, the Church [*ekklesia,* the assembly of believers in Him].

...Ephesians lifts the believer with the ascended Christ to the heavenlies where he is made a partaker of Christ's throne....

The Location of Authority

[Through] the elevation of the Lord's people with their Head, ...they are made to sit with Christ "in the heavenlies." Christ's seat is at the right hand of God. His people, therefore, occupy "with Him" the same august position. This honor is not to a chosen few, but is the portion of all those who share the resurrection of the Son of God. It is the birthright of every true believer, of every born-again child of God...

The right hand of the throne of God is the center of power of the whole universe, and the exercising of the power of the throne was committed unto the ascended Lord...

The elevation of His people with Him to the heavenlies has no other meaning than that they are made sharers...of the authority which is His. They are made to sit with Him; that is, they share His throne. To share a throne means without question to partake of the authority which it represents.

Indeed, they have been thus elevated in the plan of God, for this very purpose, that they may even now exercise, to the extent of their spiritual apprehension, authority over the powers of the air and over the conditions which those powers have brought about on the earth and are still creating through their ceaseless manipulations of the minds and circumstances of mankind.

Rebel Holders of Authority

It is necessary to state here what is commonly understood by those who carefully study the Word, that the kingdoms of this world are under the control and leadership of satanic principalities. The great head of these is, in the Gospel of John, three times acknowledged as "prince of this world" by our Lord Himself. His asserted claim to the suzerainty of the world kingdoms, made in the presence of the Lord Jesus (Luke 4:6), was not denied by Christ.

Although a rebel against the Most High and now under judgment of dispossession (John 12:31), he is still at large, and as the masses of mankind are also rebels, he maintains over them an unquestioned, because unsuspected, rule, their eyes being blinded to his dominance (2 Corinthians 4:4)....

The Divine Purpose of the Ages

The "God of the whole earth" does not purpose to tolerate forever this rebellion against His righteousness. (See Isaiah 45:23.)

God, having redeemed a people and purified them, has introduced them potentially into the heavenlies....

This purpose, present and future, is very definitely stated in Ephesians 3:9-11...as the divine will that "now" (*nun*, the present time) unto the principalities and powers in the heavenly places might be made known *through the church* the manifold wisdom of God" (3:10). The church is to be God's instrument in declaring to these rebellious and now usurping powers the divine purpose....

This is further declared to be "according to the eternal purpose of the ages which He purposed in Christ Jesus our Lord" (3:11).

...God, through all the past ages, has had in view this wonderful plan of preparing in Christ Jesus a people, chosen and called and faithful, whom He might place in these heavenly seats to rule through the ages to come.

Far Above

Christ sits far above all...

...He fills "all in all," but has chosen to do so through His Body...

Under His Feet

"Hath put all things under His feet" (1:22).

The feet are members of the Body. How wonderful to think that the least and lowest members of the Body of the Lord, those who in a sense are the very soles of the feet, are far above all the mighty forces we have been considering. Yet so it is. What need for the Church to awake to an appreciation of her mighty place of privilege. Exalted to rule over the spiritual powers of the air, how often she fails in her ministry of authority or grovels before them in fear.

Head over All

"Head over all things to the church which is His Body" (1:22). We have little grasped the force of this marvelous truth.... Let us reverse the words to bring out more clearly their deep significance: "Head to the church over all things." His being Head over all things is for the Church's sake, that the Church, His Body, may be head over all things through Him. We need to sit reverently and long before these mighty truths, that their tremendous meaning may grasp our hearts. In this attitude, the Spirit of Truth can lift us into their comprehension, which the human mind alone will always fail to compass.

The Failure of the Church

...Why, then, is there not more manifest progress? Because a head is wholly dependent upon its body for the carrying out of its plan.... The Lord Jesus...is hindered in His mighty plans and working, because His Body has failed to appreciate the deep meaning of His exaltation and to respond to the gracious impulses which He is constantly sending for its quickening.

...God help us to realize this and to fulfill our ministry through the Word both to others and to the Lord.

CHAPTER 19

HOW TO DO
MINISTRY IN THE HEAVENLIES

M any times when someone describes to me how devils are having high carnival in their lives, I give them Mac-Millan's book, and I tell them, "Read this book. And *do page 27.*" So first of all, page 27 is quoted verbatim below. I took the liberty to italicize the part that is prayer.

Quote:

Do we believe that God "hath quickened us together with Christ and hath raised us up together, and made us sit together in heavenly places in Christ Jesus" (Ephesians 2:5-6) If we do, our reaction to it will be a fervent, *"Lord, I accept Thy gracious word. I believe that Thou hast thus wrought for me. In humble faith I do now take my seat in the heavenly places in Christ Jesus at Thy right hand. Teach me how to fulfill this sacred ministry, how to exercise the authority which Thou hast entrusted to me. Train me day by day that I may attain to the full stature of the perfect man in Christ, so that in me Thy purpose of the ages may be fulfilled. Amen."*

If we are walking in the Spirit, our normal life is in the heavenlies. To secure the consciousness of this, there must be the daily acceptance of the fact. Let us, morning by morning, as one of our first acts of worship, take our seat with Christ (as suggested in the previous paragraph) and return thanks to God for all that it implies. Let us often remind ourselves that we are seated far above all the powers of the air, and that they are in subjection to us. As our faith learns to use the Name and the Authority of Jesus, we shall find the spiritual forces yielding obedience in ways that will surprise us. As we continue to abide closely in Him, our prayers for the advancement of the kingdom will become less and less the uttering of petitions and will increasingly manifest the exercise of a spiritual authority that...binds the forces of darkness....[1]

Endquote.

How I Do It

Almost every morning, I do my ministry in the heavenlies. I do it from a seated position since I am seated with Him at the right hand of the Father. At home, I do this from my comfortable prayer chair.

First, I pray the prayer which begins in Ephesians Chapter One. I start praying with verse 17, but I do not stop at the end of the chapter; I continue with Ephesians 2:1 and then skip to 2:4-6, or 7.

Here is an example of my prayer and how I rule and reign:

God of our Lord Jesus Christ, the Father of Glory,
Please give unto me the spirit of wisdom and revelation,
    in the knowledge of Him:

Let the eyes of my understanding be enlightened;
That I may know what is

> *The hope of His calling*
> *The riches of the Glory of Your inheritance in the saints.*
> *And the exceeding greatness of Your dunamis to us-ward*
> *who believe,*
> *According to your mighty power,*
>> *which You wrought in the Messiah, The Anointed One,*
>> *when you raised Him from the dead*
>> *and set Him at your own right hand in the heavenlies.*
> *F-a-a-r A-b-o-v-e*
>> *all principality, and power, and might, and dominion,*
>> *and every name that is named,*
>> *not only in this age and world, but also in that which*
>> *is to come.*

And You have put all under His feet,
And gave Him to be the Head over all to the eklesia, which is
His Body,

> *the fullness of Him that filleth all in all.*

And me, have you quickened, when I was dead, slain by my
trespasses and sins...
But God, who is rich in mercy,
For His great love wherewith He loved me,
Even when we were dead in sins,

> *Hath quickened us together with Christ,*
> *(by grace we are saved)*
> *And hath raised us up together*
> *And made us sit together in the heavenlies in Christ Jesus.*

When He quickened Him; He quickened me.

When He raised Him; He raised me.

When He seated Him; He seated me in Him.

Therefore in Him, I am seated far above all principality, power, might and dominion, and every name that is named.

And in the Name of Jesus I will now rule and reign over the powers of darkness, because the Lord told me to, in Romans 5:17. For I have received abundance of grace and of the gift of righteousness, therefore I now reign as a king in my life by One, Jesus Christ.

Kingdom of darkness, listen to me. I hold the blood of Jesus over all things pertaining to me and I forbid your having anything to do with....

From here, I follow my spirit. I start with family. Usually I name them. Then I plead the blood over myself—spirit, soul, and body. I move then to "the good works He has ordained that I should walk in" (Eph. 2:10). I name them and their locations. And the people and places adjoined to me in these good works. I cover houses, properties, vehicles, etc....

From time to time, I begin by reading the paragraph on page 27, just as MacMillan wrote it: *"Lord, I accept Thy gracious word. I believe that Thou hast thus wrought for me. In humble faith I do now take my seat in the heavenlies in Christ Jesus at Thy right hand...."*

A Place of Safety

MacMillan points out that we occupy this place in faith, humility, boldness, and courage. He writes:

But with this courage, there must be a continual and close abiding in God, a spirit that is alert to every urge and check from Him and a mind that is steeped in the Word of God....

The Panoply of God
The only place of safety is the occupation of the seat itself. It is "far above" the enemy. If the believer abides steadfastly by faith in this location, he cannot be touched.

Consequently the enemy puts forth all his "wiles" to draw him down in spirit, for once out of his seat, his authority is gone, and he is no longer dangerous, and further, he is open to attack.

At this point is seen the meaning of the message of Ephesians Chapter 6. To maintain his place against the wiles of the devil, the believer must be constantly arrayed in full armor.[2]

Smith Wigglesworth said, "There is a place in God that Satan dare not come." This is the place, seated with Him at the right hand of the Father.

Chip Brim and the Branson Tornado

On the 29th day of February, 2012, a tornado that was 400 yards wide and was on the ground for about 20 miles, tore through Branson, Missouri. It traveled east along Highway 76, the entertainment strip, damaging and destroying theaters, motels, and businesses. After wiping out much within its path, it headed straight toward Chip and Candace Brim's home.

Chip said that it sounded like a freight train as it stormed toward them at about 1:30 in the morning.

Down on the basement level of the house, which was also living quarters, Candace was pleading the blood. Chip was sitting in his seat in the heavenlies, doing exactly as described herein—reigning in his domain.

The house was shaking. The windows were heaving.

He said, "Mom, it wasn't easy, but I was doing it."

He told me how a phrase came out his mouth that he did not think of in his head.

> *"Not one shingle. Satan, you can't have one shingle."*

He repeated it over and over, "Not one shingle. Not one shingle. Satan, you can't have one shingle."

When the storm died, they went outside. Just to the south of the house, a huge tree was uprooted. Across the way, and up a little rise, businesses were badly hit and didn't reopen for months. To the north, the house next door, and the houses all the way to the corner, were badly damaged. The roofs of many were gone. *Not one shingle* was gone from the Brim's roof. And everything else was intact.

Fox News came. In their television report, they compared the badly damaged house next door to the Brim house. Panning the camera to the Brim home, they used these exact words, "Not one shingle of this house is gone."

A week or so later, I was in the insurance office that we both use. I only needed to see a clerk, but the owner of the agency came out to see me. He said, "I went to Chip's to see what kind of damage he had. Not one shingle of his house was damaged." Again he used the exact words.

Chip posted it on YouTube that very day. At this point in time, you can watch it by searching: *Chip Brim, Branson tornado.*

ABOVE THE FRAY

In corporate prayer at *Prayer Mountain in the Ozarks,* the pray-ers here and those who join us by live streaming, make it a point to be cognizant of our position in prayer. No matter what we are praying about, we call to mind, and often speak from our lips, that we are praying from our God-given position at the Father's right hand.

Once, some years back, the Spirit of the Lord warned me that some trouble was coming. He didn't tell me what it was. But He said to me, *"I want you to live above the fray."*

> *"I want you to live above the fray."*

I recognized the trouble when it came. But I had my instructions. I had the peace of God from my view above the fray.

In the mid 1980s, I noticed a pattern in severe satanic attacks against my family. So I went to Brother Hagin. He told me, based on Isaiah 54:17, "As long as you are in this world, you can't keep weapons from being formed against you, but you can keep them from prospering."

So, I did just that. I used my authority and stopped them.

Sitting in one's seat every morning, is a way to do this. With authority and the shield of faith, we can "quench all the fiery darts of the wicked one" (Ephesians 6:16).

Always remember, when you are considering Ephesians 6 and its statement about wrestling, and the prayer armor, that Chapter 6 is a part of the same Epistle that begins with the amazing revelation of our being seated with and in Christ at the right hand of the Father. Consistently see yourself seated there.

> **Col. 3:1** If ye then be risen with Christ, seek those things which are above, **where Christ sitteth on the right hand of God.**
> **Col. 3:2** Set your affection on things above, not on things on the earth.
> **Col. 3:3** For ye are dead, and your life is hid with Christ in God.
> **Col. 3:4** When Christ, who is our life, shall appear, then shall ye also appear with him in glory.

I love this wonderful instruction from Colossians. Consider that while we are seeking those things which are above, it specifically emphasizes *"where Christ sitteth on the right hand of God,"* and remember that you are seated there in Him.

---

1. John A. MacMillan, *The Authority of the Believer*, (Camp Hill, PA: Wing Spread Publishers), pp 27, 28.

2. Ibid., pp 30, 31.

Chapter 20

Praying in Tongues in the End of Days

For if I pray in an unknown tongue,
my spirit prays....

—*1 Corinthians 14:14*

Maturing in God, and living an overcoming life, is invaluably aided by an understanding that man is a three-part being.

> **1 Th. 5:23** And the very God of peace sanctify you wholly; and *I pray God* your whole spirit and soul and body be preserved blameless unto the coming of our Lord Jesus Christ.

Man is a spirit. He has a soul (mind, will, and emotions). And he lives in a body.

It is the spirit of man that is born again. It is the spirit of man that becomes a brand new creation—where all things are made new. The life and nature of God comes into the spirit of man. The love of God is shed abroad in the spirit, the heart, of man. (Romans 5:5; 2 Corinthians 5:17.)

Kenneth Hagin Ministries has published a book I highly recommend. In it are some of the lessons I first heard him teach in 1967. I think the editors took them from that seminar. Basic things, and deep things, are covered so well in the book. Its title is descriptive of what lies within its covers: *TONGUES BEYOND THE UPPER ROOM: Everything you want to know about speaking in tongues,* compiled from the teachings of Kenneth E. Hagin. The following is an excerpt:

> ...think about the amazing thing God has done for us: He has provided a way for us whereby our spirits may pray *apart* from our minds...Through this gift of speaking with tongues, our spirits can now communicate directly with God, Who is a spirit being.
>
> You see, once you get filled with the Spirit, for the first time your own spirit can talk directly to God. Before that, you could talk to God with your mind and, of course, your emotions were involved. But speaking in tongues is a means of spirit-to-Spirit communication.[1]

We rejoice in the fact, that we are given utterance in the spirit that bypasses our minds and prays the perfect will of God.

> **1 Cor. 14:14** For if I pray in an *unknown* tongue, my spirit prayeth, but my understanding is unfruitful.
> **1 Cor. 14:15** What is it then? I will pray with the spirit, and I will pray with the understanding also: I will sing with the spirit, and I will sing with the understanding also.

I can "will" to pray or sing in tongues at any time. And I can know that I am communing spirit-to-Spirit with my Father.

WHEN WE KNOW NOT HOW TO PRAY

Around the time that I received the baptism with the Holy

Spirit, there was a situation—the death of a young woman—that I did not know how to pray about in English. Deep within my spirit, I sensed a great need for prayer for her family. And I just did not know what to say. But that very week, I received a heavenly language. And because I was in a seminar where I heard excellent teaching about what I had received, I was able to enter into a prayer that I knew came from Heaven.

> **ASV**
> **Rom. 8:26** And in like manner the Spirit also helpeth our infirmity: for we know not how to pray as we ought; but the Spirit himself maketh intercession for *us* with groanings which cannot be uttered;
> **Rom. 8:27** and he that searcheth the hearts knoweth what is the mind of the Spirit, because he maketh intercession for the saints according to *the will of* God.

In 1967, when I was filled to overflowing with the Holy Spirit, the first thing I was thankful for was that I could praise Him with an unlimited vocabulary. Praising Him in English is wonderful, but after a while, the words seem insufficient. Praising Him in tongues, one can go on, and on, and on...

Praise, too, is prayer. It is communication with God.

TONGUES FOR *THE END OF DAYS*

To write about every supernatural blessing and ability that comes with tongues is impossible. But Kenneth Hagin Ministries produced a book that does an excellent job of it.

The book I am writing, and you are reading, focuses on our subject: *Praying in the End of Days.*

Now, in these times, more often than not, we do not know how to pray as we ought. And often a matter is beyond the realm of our basic authority.

Someone came to pray with us in corporate prayer at *Prayer Mountain.* At the time, Iranian President Ahmadinejad was making ludicrous threats against Israel.

That person said, "Let's just take authority over Ahmadinejad."

We couldn't. It was beyond our realm of authority.

We could not pray the prayer of faith, as in Mark 11:24, and expect results.

How could we pray? Thank God, we could pray in tongues. We could ask God for utterance, and expect effective prayer.

Sometimes we do have utterance in English. And sometimes our prayer in tongues is interspersed with English words, or phrases. This inspired utterance, in a known tongue, is also given by the Holy Spirit within our spirits.

CREATIVE WORDS

From the beginning of *Prayer Mountain in the Ozarks,* the Lord gave instructions that we are to:

1. Pray in the plans of God.
2. Stop the strategies of the enemy.

God demonstrated the laws of creation in Genesis. Repeatedly it is written, *"And God said,"* and then it was manifested. That is still the process.

God's plan, God's will, must be uttered in words. And then, from the realm of the spirit those words take on flesh; they are manifested in this physical world.

Jesus demonstrated how it works with the fig tree. Then He told us how we could do it.

Mark 11:23 For verily I say unto you, That whosoever shall say unto this mountain, Be thou removed, and be thou cast into the sea; and shall not doubt in his heart, but shall believe that those things which he saith shall come to pass; he shall have whatsoever he saith.

Recently, the Lord spoke to me during my time of fellowship with Him: *It is not come what may. It is come what you say.* (Remember, this works in the negative, as well as the positive.)

In our own lives, we often know what to pray, and what to say. But when we are working with God about world affairs, even things of the future plans of God, we often do not know what to say. Thank God, it can be said in tongues.

> *It is not come what may. It is come what you say.*

God's law of creation is still in effect. It still must be said. But the words that must be said, oft times must bypass your head. He provided the way to do it!

NO AGENDA PRAYING

At the end of 2014, we received a new prayer assignment for corporate prayer.

(When I say "we" I mean the corporate pray-ers that join in prayer from this base: *Prayer Mountain in the Ozarks.* As of this writing, twice weekly, pray-ers meet here in the chapel for corporate prayer. On Wednesday at noon CST we stream the meeting. Many faithful pray-ers from around the world join us live via Internet. Many others join us later by watching the archives. They report that the anointing is just as strong on the archives. On Sunday at 3 o'clock, we also meet, but we do not stream. A few years back, those who join from around the world began to call themselves WWP's, in the emails they sent us. *World Wide Pray-ers.* Several thousand come each year to pray together in our *Autumn Assembly of Prayer* here in Branson.)

For some time, the thought that we need to increase prayer weighed upon me. *Twenty-four seven prayer.* But how do we go about it? As I contemplated how to do it, these thoughts came:

> *It wouldn't really work to increase prayer here on the mountain to 24/7. We would just have a bunch of tired people. These faithful pray-ers already travel long distances to come out here twice a week for corporate prayer. And besides, this needs to be united prayer from a far wider scope. It needs to come from around the world. From the World Wide Pray-ers.*

GOD-GIVEN ORDERS!

A plan began to form within me. Direction came.

Make a round 24-hour clock. Divide it into 30-minute pie-shaped segments. Prayer warriors will sign up to pray during one of those 30-minute segments. The prayer is to be in the Spirit. In tongues. You are to pray with "no agenda."

No agenda! No pre-determined subject of our prayers.

(That kind of prayer is for another time in the day.) *In this prayer, one will offer one's self totally to the Holy Spirit to pray what God wants prayed.* He has need for certain utterances to be made in the earth.

A prayer captain will keep track of the 30-minute segments. The clock will be kept according to CST, however those volunteering from Australia, for example, will advise the prayer captain of the segment they will pray. She will convert it to our "clock."

For those who, because of their life's pattern, cannot keep the regimen of a certain time period; they can be "floaters." They too will contact the prayer captain, and advise her that they will pray 30 minutes a day at the time their schedules provide.

The Word

Of course, we base everything on the written Word. Every Scripture as to the Body's authority and position in prayer is applicable. I particularly thought of when we know not how to pray as we ought (Romans 8:26,27). And also how the eyes of the Lord run to and fro in the earth searching for those through whom He can show Himself strong (2 Chronicles 16:9).

On Wednesday, November 19, 2014, I prepared to share this new assignment with the noontime corporate prayer meeting. When I opened my Bible the first thing that morning, it fell open to a passage I used to preach from 30 years ago. First Chronicles 12. It is the Lord's assessment of the merits of the men in David's army. Instantly, I knew the Lord drew my attention to that passage for us now.

For He told me many years ago, *As nations raise up an Air Force, I am raising up a Prayer Force.* And I knew the attributes God pointed out in David's army are those He wants in His Prayer Force today. I read First Chronicles 12 in the King James, and then in the *Amplified.* And I realized that He was promoting us. We were being organized into battle array. We were taking a higher step. We had a new assignment.

David's army was preparing the way for David to become King. We are to prepare the way for the coming of the King of Kings.

UNITY FOR THE GLORY

I shared these things with my good friend, Sharon Daugherty, Pastor and Co-founder of Victory Christian Center in Tulsa. She instantly witnessed with the prayer assignment and said they would join us. Then she brought out something I had not thought of.

She said, "Billye, this is how we can work in unity for the glory!"

> **John 17:20** Neither pray I for these alone, but for them also which shall believe on me through their word;
> **John 17:21** That they all may be one; as thou, Father, *art* in me, and I in thee, **that they also may be one in us: that the world may believe that thou hast sent me.**
> **John 17:22 And the glory which thou gavest me I have given them; that they may be one, even as we are one:**
> **John 17:23** I in them, and thou in me, **that they may be made perfect in one; and that the world may know** that thou hast sent me, and hast loved them, as thou hast loved me.

I also know, that Romans 8:26, 27, which we have quoted above, is tied to Creation's groaning for the manifestation of the sons of God, and the glory that shall be revealed in us (Romans 8:18-27).

GREAT HAPPENINGS

Consider prayerfully this prophecy given through Kenneth E. Hagin in The Winter Bible Seminar of 1997:

Speaking by the Spirit,
*   not just speaking words out of your own mind or thinking,*
*   but speaking by the Spirit;*
Words that are inspired by the Spirit of God;
Words that well up from within you, out of your spirit,
*   given to you by the Holy Spirit.*
Those words, spoken boldly bring forth great happenings.

Speaking by the Spirit,
And so the Glory of God shall come into manifestation.
And some will see it like a cloud that hangs over the heads of the people.
Others may not see anything, but they sense the mighty move of His Spirit.

Speaking by His Spirit,
Yielding your tongue unto the Holy Ghost,
Taking time to pray in the Spirit,
Taking time to pray in other tongues,
*   will get you tuned up, will edify you,*

and get your tongue hooked up to your spirit,
so that then, He who dwells in your spirit
can give you utterance.
Then He takes over.
And you speak out what He says, not what you think.
Speak out what He wants.

And so, the Spirit of Seeing and the Spirit of Knowing
into a greater manifestation shall come.
All of these,
All nine of these manifestations,
all of them worketh that one and the selfsame Spirit.
And, at the same time, "the inspirational gifts,"
men, women, speaking by the Spirit,
by Prophecy, inspired utterance,
by Tongues and interpretations,
Shall bring forth marvelous statements,
And bring to pass and bring into being
in this sense realm
where men can see and know,
The operation of the Spirit of God,
And the manifestation of the Spirit of God,
And the demonstration of the Spirit of God.
So rejoice ye, and be ye glad.

---

1. Kenneth E. Hagin, *TONGUES BEYOND THE UPPER ROOM*, (Tulsa, OK: Rhema Bible Church, 2007), pp 151,152.

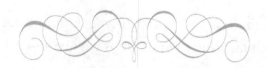

Chapter 21

Praying the Mysteries of God

The English word 'mystery' is a transliteration of the Greek word *musterion,* which means a sacred secret."[1] How intriguing that the New Testament identifies certain subjects as *mysteries* of God—and the plans of God so specified as mysteries are front and center in the happenings of the end of days.

> **KJV**
> **1 Cor. 14:2** For he that speaketh in an *unknown* tongue speaketh not unto men, but unto God: for no man understandeth *him;* howbeit in the spirit he speaketh mysteries.

This one verse is so full of revelation. It tells born again believers that:

1. There are mysteries.
2. We can speak about them.
3. Our speaking is directly to God.
4. There is a supernatural language in which to speak.

God needs the body of Christ to speak about these mysteries. How exhilarating to know that we are given a secret language in which to do so.

Now we will just touch upon some of the topics the New Testament identifies as *mysteries.*

THE MYSTERY OF THE CHURCH (*ECCLESIA*, ASSEMBLY) THE BODY OF CHRIST

The great "hidden mystery" is that of the *ecclesia* (Greek for "called out assembly") but usually translated "church."

> **Rom. 16:25** Now to him that is of power to stablish you according to my gospel, and the preaching of Jesus Christ, according to **the revelation** of **the mystery, which was kept secret since the world began,**
> **Rom. 16:26** But now is made manifest....
>
> **Eph. 3:3** How that **by revelation he made known unto me the mystery;** (as I wrote afore in few words,
> **Eph. 3:4** Whereby, when ye read, ye may understand my knowledge in **the mystery of Christ**)
> **Eph. 3:5** Which in other ages was not made known unto the sons of men, as it is now revealed...
> **Eph. 3:6** That the Gentiles should be fellowheirs, and of the same body, and partakers of his promise in Christ by the gospel...
> **Eph. 3:9** And to make all *men* see what is the fellowship of **the mystery, which from the beginning of the world hath been hid in God,** who created all things by Jesus Christ:
> **Eph. 3:10** To the intent that now unto the principalities and powers in heavenly *places* might be known by the church the manifold wisdom of God,
> **Eph. 3:11** According to the eternal purpose which he purposed in Christ Jesus our Lord:

This mystery was concealed until the time for it to be revealed. It was not revealed to the Old Testament Prophets. It was not revealed in the Four Gospels. It was revealed, in the timing of God, to the Apostle Paul.

Paul said of the gospel he preached, "I neither received of man, neither was I taught it, but by the revelation of Jesus Christ" (Gal. 1:11,12).

I remember how engrossed I was when I first heard Kenneth E. Hagin's teaching entitled "Paul's Revelation." My heart somehow *saw* into the Lord's early dealings with the Apostle who wrote so much of the New Testament. Kenneth Hagin pointed out that Paul was virtually isolated—away from James and the Twelve—for 17 plus years while his revelation came (Gal. 1:11-24).

Brother Hagin said, "If you had read only the Four Gospels, you wouldn't even know why Jesus came. You think you would, because you have read all the New Testament, but you would not. You wouldn't know that He defeated Satan and gave authority over him to you. You wouldn't know about the new creation man...."

> **1 Cor. 2:7** But we speak **the wisdom of God in a mystery,** *even* **the hidden** *wisdom*, **which God ordained before the world unto our glory:**
> **1 Cor. 2:8** Which none of the princes of this world knew: for had they known *it*, they would not have crucified the Lord of glory.
>
> **Col. 1:26** *Even* **the mystery which hath been hid from ages and from generations,** but now is made manifest to his saints:
> **Col. 1:27** To whom God would make known what *is* the riches of **the glory of this mystery** among the Gentiles; **which is Christ in you, the hope of glory:**

Eph. 5:25 ... Christ also loved the church, and gave himself for it [her];
Eph. 5:26 That he might sanctify and cleanse it [her] with the washing of water by the word,
Eph. 5:27 That he might present it [her] to himself a glorious church, not having spot, or wrinkle, or any such thing; but that it [she] should be holy and without blemish...
Eph. 5:30 For we are members of his body, of his flesh, and of his bones...
Eph. 5:32 This is a great mystery: but I speak concerning Christ and the church.

Paul's revelation was that of a body prepared for the Master. The risen Lord is its Head. The *ecclesia* is His body. (See John 17:20-26; Rom. 12:5; 1 Cor. 12:12-27.)

Those who believe in the risen Savior, and confess Him as Lord, are born again. They become brand new creations—a brand new species—which never before existed. The inner man, the spirit, is born again. Within the spirit man, the real man, old things pass away—all things become new. (See 2 Cor. 5:17.)

> *The door is open to the Gentiles (nations) as well as to the Jews...*

The door is open to the Gentiles (nations) as well as to the Jews—but in the body of Christ there is neither Jew nor Gentile. The two are one in Him.

The new believer is *born from above*. The margin of my reference Bible says that the word translated *again* in John 3:3, 7 is actually *from above*. Like Jesus, our Head, the believer is from above and not of this world (John 8:23). Heavenly Jerusalem is our mother, our birthplace (Gal. 3:23). Our citizenship, now and forever, is in heaven (Phil. 3:20). The new creation believer operates as an ambassador from heaven to earth (2 Cor. 5:20). Like earthly ambassadors the believer operates by the laws of the home country (Romans 8:2).

I sometimes say, "I am an alien from another planet." I carry a U.S. passport, but my citizenship is in heaven.

Authority is given to the body of Christ. In His death, burial, resurrection and ascension, Jesus made an open show of His triumph over Satan and his followers (Col 4:15).

When God quickened the crucified Lord, He quickened His body. When He raised the Head, He raised the body. When He seated the Lord Jesus at His right hand—the center of authority in all of creation—He seated His body in Him (Col. 2:12, 13; Eph. 1:19-2:7). From there the body is to rule and reign in this life (See Romans 5:17, Amplified.) The body is to carry out God's will on the earth.

> *The body is to carry out God's will on the earth.*

Each believer is given the Name of Jesus, the blood of Jesus, the Word of God, and through these the kingdom of darkness must obey even the youngest in natural years, or the newest born again babe in Christ. (See Mark 16:17; Rev. 12:11.)

The Greater One indwells each believer (1 John 4:4). Each member of the Lord's body is a Temple of the indwelling Holy Spirit (1 Cor. 3:16; 6:19; 2 Cor. 6:16).

The Love of God is shed abroad in the spirit of every new creature (Romans 5:5).

The Glory of God is within each believer, and degree-by-degree it will eventually "glorify" that new creation until that one is in the image of the Master (Col 1:26, 27; 2 Cor. 3:18).

This is a very limited summary of a vast treasure trove of the access, authority, blessing, gifts, grace, glory, righteous-ness, etc., afforded each member of the body of Christ. To go into it adequately here would require that we print in entire-ty all the Epistles to the church.

Suffice it to say, this is a great mystery.

THE MYSTERY OF THE CATCHING AWAY AND GLORIFICATION OF THE BODY OF CHRIST

KJV
1 Cor. 15:51 Behold, **I shew you a mystery;** We shall not all sleep, but we shall all be changed,
1 Cor. 15:52 In a moment, in the twinkling of an eye, at the last trump: for the trumpet shall sound, and the dead shall be raised incorruptible, and we shall be changed.
1 Cor. 15:53 For this corruptible must put on incorrup-tion, and this mortal *must* put on immortality.

(See also 1 Thessalonians 4:13-18.)

THE MYSTERY OF INIQUITY

KJV
2 Th. 2:3 Let no man deceive you by any means: for *that day shall not come,* except there come a falling away first, and that man of sin be revealed, the son of perdition;
2 Th. 2:4 Who opposeth and exalteth himself above all that is called God, or that is worshipped; so that he as God sitteth in the temple of God, shewing himself that he is God...

2 Th. 2:6 And now ye know what withholdeth that he might be revealed in his time.

2 Th. 2:7 For **the mystery of iniquity** doth already work: only he who now letteth *will let,* until he be taken out of the way.

2 Th. 2:8 And then shall that Wicked be revealed, whom the Lord shall consume with the spirit of his mouth, and shall destroy with the brightness of his coming:

ASV

2 Th. 2:3 let no man beguile you in any wise: for *it will not be,* except the falling away come first, and the man of sin be revealed, the son of perdition,

2 Th. 2:4 he that opposeth and exalteth himself against all that is called God or that is worshipped; so that he sitteth in the temple of God, setting himself forth as God.

2 Th. 2:6 And now ye know that which restraineth, to the end that he may be revealed in his own season.

2 Th. 2:7 For **the mystery of lawlessness** doth already work: only *there is* one that restraineth now, until he be taken out of the way.

2 Th. 2:8 And then shall be revealed the lawless one, whom the Lord Jesus shall slay with the breath of his mouth, and bring to nought by the manifestation of his coming;

On April 24, 1967, as a young wife and mother in my late 20s, I was baptized with the Holy Spirit with the evidence of speaking in tongues. With the Author of the scriptures now in greater evidence in my life, I began to wake up to wonderful biblical truths. One was the fact that I was living in prophetic days.

Less than two months later, in June 1967, in the miraculous Six Day War, Jerusalem was reunited. The Jews got back biblical sites where their ancestors had worshiped and reigned thousands of years before. Scriptures prophesying their return to the Promised Land were being fulfilled before the eyes of the world.

About this time I began to hear guesses as to the identity of the antichrist. Each theory had a formula that backed up its conclusion. Often it had to do with the letters of the suspect's name somehow associated with 666.

The same people who took me to hear Kenneth E. Hagin, under whose ministry I received the baptism with the Holy Spirit, took me to hear Dr. Hilton Sutton. Dr. Sutton, who later became one of my mentors, was a dynamic teacher of prophecy until his passing at age 88 in 2012. But he was especially exciting to listen to in the prophetic summer of 1967.

In his seminars, I heard him say that the identity of the antichrist could not be made known before the rapture of the body of Christ—and that all such guessing is futile. Dr. Sutton taught, expounding on this passage, that a restraining force is holding back the antichrist and his revelation until it is taken out of the way. That hindering force is the Spirit indwelt body of Christ.

> *That hindering force is the Spirit indwelt body of Christ.*

Therefore, we are to hinder, to hold back, to restrain the antichrist and spirits of antichrist, until we are caught up to meet the Lord in the air (1 Thess. 4:13-18).

One way (not the only way) we can do that is praying in tongues as First Corinthians 14:2 reveals. For the activity of the antichrist is one of the identifiable mysteries: *the mystery of iniquity.*

THE MYSTERY OF ISRAEL

David Baron calls Romans 9-11 a "wonderful section of the Epistles to the Romans."[2]

These three chapters are literally a book within a Book speaking of God's plan for Israel in a Letter to the Church.

The Lord identifies that plan as one of His *mysteries*. He emphasizes that He does not want the church to be *"ignorant of this mystery"* and that to do so is to be conceited (Romans 11:25).

Baron was born a Jew in Russia in 1855 and trained in the best rabbinical schools. After his conversion to Christianity he became a prolific teacher and author. The following is a comment on these chapters and particularly on Romans 11:25-29 from his book, *Israel in the Plan of God*.[3]

> ...the covenant relationship into which He entered with them is an indissoluble one, and His original purpose in the call and election of this nation shall yet be realized...in that wonderful section of his Epistle to the Romans...in spite of all that has happened, God's purpose in the election of this nation stands; that the blindness or hardness which has befallen Israel is only a *partial* one—both to its extent and in its duration—that "all Israel shall be saved," when "the Redeemer" is manifested to them... "for the gifts and the calling of God are without repentance" or change of mind on His part, i.e. IRREVOCABLE."

FINALLY...CONCERNING THE MYSTERIES

You can find what the New Testament calls mysteries by checking for the words *mystery* or *mysteries* in a good concordance. A concordance on ones computer makes that an easy task. You can pray about these with your understanding, of course. But know that when you have yielded your vessel, your tongue, to praying in the Spirit, you may be praying about any one of these identifiable mysteries, speaking to God the Father, the utterances He gives you to be spoken into the earth. (See elsewhere in this book where I have written on *Praying in Tongues.*)

When you pray in tongues, unknown to you, you may be praying about any one of the members in the body of Christ, or a congregation, or the entire body... You may be praying about the Rapture... You may be praying to stop a strategic move of the spirits of antichrist... You may be praying for Israel, its people, or its Land. For it is certain that you are speaking to God Himself concerning the *mysteries....*

---

1.   *The Companion Bible,* Notes and Appendixes by E. W. Bullinger, (Grand Rapids, MI, Kregal Publications), Appendix 193.

2.   David Baron, *Israel in the Plan of God,* (Grand Rapids, MI: Kregel Publications, 1983), p 44.

3.   Ibid., pp 43, 44.

Chapter 22

Praying for Nations and Leaders

I exhort therefore, that, first of all, supplications,
prayers, intercessions, and giving of thanks,
be made for all men;
For kings, and for all that are in authority;
that we may lead a quiet and peaceable life
in all godliness and honesty.
For this is good and acceptable in the sight
of God our Saviour;
Who will have all men to be saved, and to come
unto the knowledge of the truth.

— First Timothy 2:1-4

I am sure that if Christians had obeyed this exhortation, our world would not be in the condition it is today.

"*First of all....*" First of all, before we pray for anything else, we are to pray for the leaders.

How do we pray for them?

We can begin by holding up this verse before the Lord.

AUTHORITY IN PRAYER FOR LEADERS

We can use our God-given authority that this verse, and our place at the Father's right hand, gives us.

Satan is not omnipresent, as God is. Satan cannot be in all places at once. Therefore, most people on earth have never known targeting by the chief terrorist himself.

Who has known it?

The archenemy spends his limited time on: Presidents and Kings. Heads of State. Heads of ministries. Persons of wealth and influence.

I believe the admonition to pray, "first of all, for those in authority," applies to spiritual authority as well as civil authority.

Often times, when a spiritual leader stands strong against Satan's wiles, the evil one attacks the minister's family.

You and I have a sort of inherent right of authority, in the spiritual realm, concerning our own leaders.

For instance, I have a right to come against the demons that would bother my Mayor, my Congressperson, my Governor, and my President. And concerning spiritual authority, my Pastor, my Teacher, etc.

We do not have authority over people. Our authority is over demons. See the preceeding the chapters on exercising authority in prayer.

INTERCESSION

In intercession, we take the place of another. We stand in the gap. The very next verse says:

1 Tim. 2:5 For *there is* one God, and one mediator between God and men, the man Christ Jesus;

In Him, Christ the Mediator, the Great Intercessor, we intercede and expect His help. We can lift those in authority to the Lord.

After my husband moved to heaven in 1986, when I prayed about what to do, the Lord directed me to *Study Hebrew in the Land. I am going to place you close to the Jews.*

He did just that. He led me to study at an outstanding language school, Ulpan Akiva. Shulamith Katznelson, the school's head, was twice nominated for the Nobel Peace Prize for founding it. She became my close friend. It was through her that He first placed me close to so many Jews, including leaders. Her family members, Shulamith included, were leaders in the miraculous rebirth of Israel.

> *"Study Hebrew in the Land. I am going to place you close to the Jews."*

Her brother, Shmuel Tamir, was a prominent Israeli Independence fighter, lawyer, Knesset member, and Minister of Justice in the government of Menachem Begin.

He passed away after an illness in 1987. His body, wrapped in an Israeli flag, lay in state for a few hours in front of a government building.

Shulamith invited me to stand with the family. I was standing there with them when Israel's Joint Prime Ministers, Shamir and Peres, greeted the family. The Prime Ministers were so close, I could have reached out and touched them.

Immediately, I knew in my spirit that God had placed me there to pray for them. And immediately, He showed me how to do it. What Rachel Teafatiller sometimes did came to my mind. So I did it.

Rachel said that she "put people in a basket and lifted them to the Lord." I imagined that I held a basket in my hands. And that in the basket were the two Prime Ministers of Israel, the apple of God's eye. Then I lifted the basket to the Lord. All this was done silently. Not even my lips moved.

We can lift leaders to the Lord, and expect His help.

WHAT ABOUT LEADERS WE DON'T LIKE?

Rome, the great iron beast, was the authority over Israel when Paul wrote Timothy. As nearly as I can determine, Nero, the most evil of all Roman leaders, was in power. And we find no disqualification of any leaders in the "first of all" prayer instruction.

> *Spirit led prayer is always the best prayer.*

Spirit-led prayer is always the best prayer.

Make sure you are in a position to be led by the Spirit. Otherwise we just pray in the flesh, and as it is written, flesh profiteth nothing.

From time to time, the Spirit has led us to pray according to Job 33:14-17, that the Lord would give a leader, or leaders, dreams and night visions.

But we don't make that a rule. With the things of God, we don't make hard and fast rules—we follow the Spirit of God.

PRAYING FOR AN AWAKENING

Sunday, June 29, 2008, at our 3 o'clock prayer meeting in the chapel at *Prayer Mountain in the Ozarks,* God interrupted us. We had been praying about the upcoming election. His Presence filled the room. And He shook us. The word of the Lord came through my lips:

> *One thing will save America.*
> *And it is not the election.*
> **It is an awakening to God.**
> *One thing will avail for Israel and the nations.*
> **It is an awakening to God.**

Silenced in our petitions. Even rebuked. Our hearts listened for more. More words came. And at the same time, Spirit-inspired thoughts sped through my mind.

The best person in the world could be elected President, and it wouldn't help if America did not awaken to God. American history. The Great Awakening. The part of prayer in the Great Awakening. Study.

So that's what I did. I studied.

Much of what I learned, I wrote to my partners as I was learning. We published those partner letters in a book entitled, *Letters to Partners in the Service of the Lord.*[1]

PRAYING IN TONGUES

This is most often the best way to pray. We just have to be more disciplined to do it. Prayer changes things. If we want change, we must pray.

HOW JEWS CAN PRAY FOR ISRAEL

You may have noticed that I left out 2 Chronicles 7:14.

I wouldn't be dogmatic about this, but I believe that promise is specifically for Israel. Our New Testament instruction and equipment is specific and entirely sufficient for the new creation body of Christ.

The passage in Chronicles happened during the Feast of Tabernacles just after the First Temple was finished, and the Ark of the Covenant of the Lord was moved into the Holy of Holies. It may even have been a Jubilee. The Feast was celebrated seven days. Consider the entire context in the light of this great event:

> **2 Chr. 7:12** And the LORD appeared to Solomon by night, and said unto him, I have heard thy prayer, and have chosen this place to myself for an house of sacrifice.
> **2 Chr. 7:13** If I shut up heaven that there be no rain, or if I command the locusts to devour the land, or if I send pestilence among my people;
> **2 Chr. 7:14** If my people, which are called by my name, shall humble themselves, and pray, and seek my face, and turn from their wicked ways; then will I hear from heaven, and will forgive their sin, and will heal their land.
> **2 Chr. 7:15** Now mine eyes shall be open, and mine ears attent unto the prayer *that is made* in this place.
> **2 Chr. 7:16** For now have I chosen and sanctified this house, that my name may be there for ever: and mine eyes and mine heart shall be there perpetually.

Israel had been looking for *"HaMakom," The Place,* ever since God promised there was only one place they were to worship—the place He chose to place His Name there. The LORD confirmed to Solomon that they had found *HaMakom, The Place.* See my book, *Jerusalem, Above and Below.*[2]

The prayer authorized in 2 Chronicles 7:14 is limited to prayer made in a certain place, and really, to a certain people, the Jews.

We have a better covenant, based on better promises.

ARIEL SHARON

I am a witness to 2 Chronicles 7:14 working for Ariel Sharon, one of the great Jewish leaders in the rebirth of Israel. I had been in his presence, off and on, for several years when he summoned me to his office that auspicious day, September 11, 2000.

Two days before, he spoke to my tour group of 26 people at the Likkud headquarters in Tel Aviv, where he was leader of the opposition.

He told our group, "Jerusalem is in the greatest trouble it has been in since the establishment of the Modern State of Israel."

Prime Minister Ehud Barak had offered sovereignty over the Temple Mount to Yasser Arafat.

As I went out the door of the building I told him we were going to Ariel (the capital of what the world calls the west bank) and that tomorrow we were going to pray at *Alon Moreh* where God appeared to Abraham. (King James translates it "the plain of Moreh." But it is an *alon,* an oak tree, on the Mountain of Abraham.)

Sharon said to me, "I built Ariel. It is named for me, Ariel."

Prayer at *Alon Moreh* was exceedingly powerful. Supernatural things happened all around us. Strong winds encircled us. Three groups of 11 eagles each flew below us, and then became a group of 33, and flew over our heads. We were instructed to read passages from the Bible—Ezekiel 36 and Genesis 12:1-3. A handsome young Israeli, recently returned from IDF duty, read God's promise to Abraham in Hebrew. I cannot describe the happenings of that day as we prayed for Israel in her time of trouble. But there are 25 reliable witnesses to them.

When we got back to the hotel in Ariel, the owners swarmed me, "Arik wants to see you. Arik wants to see you."

A very long story short, the next day, an Israeli friend drove Lucy McKee and me to Sharon's office.

It was a hubbub of activity. For it was the date upon which, seven years before, Arafat vowed that he would unilaterally declare a Palestinian state.

It had been seven years since September 13, 1993, and the handshakes on the White House lawn between Israeli Prime Minister Rabin, Arafat, and President Clinton.

The world wanted to know what Sharon would do about it. Diplomats and the Press crowded the outer office. I recognized a former Israeli Ambassador to the United States when he came out from being with Sharon. Then I looked around and saw the people waiting to get in.

I had just had the thought that we would be there all day,

when Mr. Gissin, Sharon's senior advisor, came to the door and motioned for us to come in. He ushered us to an inner office where Sharon sat at a long table. I was asked to sit across from Sharon. Lucy sat next to me.

After saying, "Shalom," Sharon said not another word.

Silence.

The only thing I know to say is, the Spirit of the Lord came down on me. I gave him a scripture in English. He asked Mr. Gissin to get him his Tanach. His well worn Bible. He read the scripture in Hebrew.

Silence.

Again the Spirit of the Lord came down upon me. And I found myself telling him about what happened at *Alon Moreh*. Wind, eagles, scripture, and all.

He turned to Ezekiel 36 and began to read in Hebrew.

Mr. Gissin asked, "How much are you going to read?

"Ze whole chapter." And he read it all—in Hebrew. Every once in a while he moved his hand over the written page, looked up, and said in English, "Dis is how it is."

Lucy's eyes filled with silent tears that spilled out over the bottom lids like a stream over a low water dam. Sharon later called her the lady with eyes like pools.

After he finished, he said, "Did you know that the next chapter, is the chapter upon which we founded the Modern State of Israel?"

And he proceeded to read all of Chapter 37, the Dry Bones Chapter.

Then he picked up the phone and ordered coffee and tea.

He looked at us and said very simply, "The only thing I

know to do, is to go up on the Temple Mount and pray."

Lucy said, "Well..."

He knew it could cause an International uproar, and even war. But he knew 2 Chronicles 7:14. And he knew it required going to *HaMakom,* The Place.

When we got home to America, he actually telephoned Lucy and Lynne at the Hammond's house in Minneapolis, and me at my house in Missouri. He told us that he was going through with it, and he asked us to pray.

On September 28, 2000, against all political advice, he did just that.

And against all odds, everyone said he could not win, he became the next Prime Minister of Israel. Rabbis said that it was because he went to the Mount to pray.

He did many good things. But then, the enemy of God and of Israel, deceived him into the mistake of pushing the Jews out of Gaza. The same Rabbis said that this act led to his demise.

None-the-less, I witnessed how a Jewish leader acted on Israel's covenant promise in 2 Chronicles 7:14. And I saw that it worked.

If Israeli leaders today would pray in line with that promise, it would work.

If we Christians pray in line with what God promised us, it will work.

---

1. Dr. Billye Brim, *Letters to Partners,* (Branson, MO: Billye Brim Ministries, 2012).

2. Ibid., *JERUSALEM, Above and Below.*

CHAPTER 23

HOW YOU CAN PRAY FOR ISRAEL AND JERUSALEM

Israel, and especially Jerusalem, is the center of the earth in the mind of God. Therefore, Israel and Jerusalem hold supreme importance for our subject—*Prayer in the End of Days.* They are forever the "apple of God's eye" and pivotal to His plans for earth and its peoples.

> **Deut. 32:8** When the most High divided to the nations their inheritance, when he separated the sons of Adam, he set the bounds of the people according to the number of the children of Israel.
> **Deut. 32:9** For the LORD'S portion *is* his people; Jacob *is* the lot of his inheritance.
> **Deut. 32:10** He found him in a desert land, and in the waste howling wilderness; he led him about, he instructed him, he kept him as the apple of his eye.

An old German writer called the 32nd Chapter of Deuteronomy, *God's Manifesto* in relation to the Jewish nation.

David Baron, in his book *Israel in the Plan of God,* called it "a condensed...comprehensive prophecy, setting forth...the dealings of God with that nation—past, present, and future." Commenting on verses 8-10 he said, "Here we...learn the great truth, confirmed...in other Scriptures, that the land and people of Israel were from the very beginning the appointed centre in the counsel of God for His governmental dealings with the nations of the earth."[1]

Zechariah also calls Israel "the apple of God's eye." And identifies Jerusalem as the touchstone in God's judgment of the nations.

> **Zech. 2:8** For thus saith the LORD of hosts; After the glory hath he sent me unto the nations which spoiled you: for he that toucheth you toucheth the **apple** of his eye.
>
> **Zech. 12:2** Behold, I will make Jerusalem a cup of trembling unto all the people round about, when they shall be in the siege both against Judah *and* against Jerusalem.
> **Zech. 12:3** And in that day will I make Jerusalem a burdensome stone for all people: all that burden themselves with it shall be cut in pieces, though all the people of the earth be gathered together against it.

The Bible often speaks of "a *cup* of judgment" from which nations must drink. The word translated *cup* in verse 2 is more literally a *basin*—therefore indicating an unusually large judgment. Judgment of the nations is based squarely on what they say and do about Israel and Jerusalem. (See my mini-book, *Judgment of the Nations for How They Treat Israel.*)[2]

It is important to note Deuteronomy 32:9, "*Jacob* is the lot of His inheritance." When the Bible calls Israel "Jacob," it refers to the physical descendants of the first Jew, Abraham. It doesn't call them Abraham, for he had other sons. It doesn't call them Isaac, for he had another son. It calls them Jacob, for all Jacob's sons were the origins of the twelve tribes of Israel.

Israel is the LORD's portion—separated as a nation from the nations. The Body of Christ is the Lord's portion taken out from among every nation, people, and tongue.

WHY DO WE PRAY FOR JERUSALEM?

Because the Lord told us to!

> **Psa. 122:6** Pray for the peace of Jerusalem: they shall prosper that love thee.

He told us that *we are to pray*—and He told us specifically *what to pray:*

PRAY FOR THE *PEACE* OF JERUSALEM...

Many lovers of Israel pray for the peace of Jerusalem without realizing what the LORD means when He says, "Pray for the *peace* of Jerusalem."

The original Hebrew text says to pray for the *shalom* of Jerusalem. *Shalom* does not mean the absence of war. The literal meaning of *shalom* is: *the peace that comes from being whole.* To pray for the *shalom* of Jerusalem is to pray for its *wholeness.*

You can better understand God's instruction with a little knowledge of Hebrew—the original language of The Old Testament. You can easily see it in these quotes from Edward Horowitz's text for the study of modern Hebrew, *How the Hebrew Language Grew.*[3]

The Hebrew Root has Three Consonants—usually
We now come to the central theme of all word build-

ing in Hebrew; it is the central rhythm of the whole, vast, far-flung structure of the Hebrew language.

This is it:

Practically all words in Hebrew go back to a root—and this root must have in it three consonants. You can do anything you want to the root: you can use it in any verb form or tense, you can turn it into any one of ten or twenty or more nouns. You can make it an adjective, adverb, preposition, or what you will.... *No matter what you do you will always see staring you in the face the three consonants of the root. You can never escape them.*

And equally important:

No matter what you do with the root, no matter into what word you turn it—*that word must carry in it something of the meaning of the root....*

Mr. Horowitz illustrates this word building as a wheel. The three-letter root word is the hub of the wheel. Vowel sounds weaving in and out among the consonants of the root create other words. These words are in the spokes of the wheel.

When I ask people what is the most well known Hebrew word, they usually answer, *"Hallelujah."* Yet another word is much more widely used. It is the word *Amen.*

Herein I have reproduced Horowitz's word wheel for the root *Amen* אמן. Its literal meaning is: *May this prayer come true.* Circling around the hub are words from this root. Notice how many of the words describe what it takes to make a prayer come true. *Truth,* (God's Word). *Faith. Believed. Right Hand,* (The right hand of God signifies His power). A family of words growing from one root often illustrates a particular biblical truth.

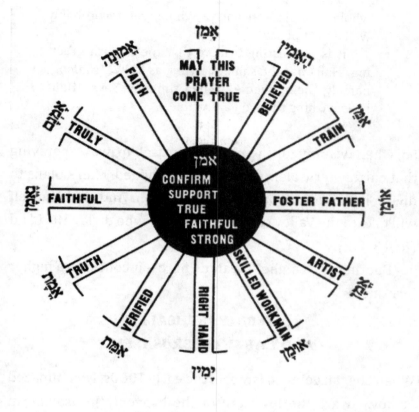

Here's what Horowitz says about another family of words. And remember, he is writing primarily to Jewish students:

שלם — BE WHOLE, COMPLETE

It probably never occurred to you and it may faintly amuse you to know that when someone says to you inquiringly "מא שלום לך" ["*What is your peace?*"] —he is actually asking you whether you are whole, complete, in one piece. They want assurance that no part of you—fingers, toes, legs, arms, etc. is missing or broken. The root meaning of our familiar greeting word שלום (*shalom*) is שלם (*shalem*) whole, complete. If you're whole, you're probably well and at peace.

It is interesting to note that the English greeting "Hail," has the same meaning as שלום (*shalom*), namely, "being whole." When someone says, "Hail" he is wishing that you are whole.

So, when we pray for the peace of Jerusalem, we are praying that earthly Jerusalem be whole—undivided. Man's plans to divide it are not according to God's plan. And God Himself will take to the Valley of Judgment those who divide His Land (Joel 3:1, 2).

But there is a higher meaning here—it concerns a higher Jerusalem.

HEAVENLY JERUSALEM AND EARTHLY JERUSALEM

When I began going to Israel in the early 1980s, I was amazed at how aware the Jews are of the heavenly Jerusalem. In shops everywhere I saw paintings of both cities, the heavenly Jerusalem painted just above the earthly.

The Hebrew name for the heavenly Jerusalem is *Yerushalayim shel ma'alah,* "Jerusalem on High." Many Jews hold it in their consciousness. And they believe that it parallels the earthly Jerusalem, which they call *Yerushalayim shel matah,* "Jerusalem that is below."

This surprised me. For I found more in the New Testament about "Jerusalem that is above," than in the Old Testament. And yet, I saw that its reality was more in the minds of Israel's Jews than in the thinking of Christians.

One day I went into one of the four oldest synagogues in Jerusalem. And there, just above the ark, which holds the Torah scrolls, heavenly Jerusalem was painted as a menorah—a seven-branched lampstand—in the clouds above earthly Jerusalem. This symbolized that Light comes from Jerusalem on High to Jerusalem below. The friendly white-bearded rabbi was from New York. So I asked him how they knew so much about Jerusalem on high.

"Moses told us," he said. "He went there."

Well, it dawned on me; *I suppose if someone could go there now, surely Moses in all those days with God did ascend the Heavenly Mount.*

I asked the rabbi if he could show me in the scriptures.

He gave me one of the Psalms of Ascent, the songs they sang as they went up to Jerusalem.

> **KJV**
> **Psa. 122:3** Jerusalem is builded as a city that is compact together:

He expounded on the upper and lower cities being builded together.

Young's Literal Translation shows this so well:

> **YLT**
> **Psa. 122:3** Jerusalem — the builded one — [Is] as a city that is joined to itself together.

I have learned much from David Baron. After becoming a Christian he was a prolific teacher and author. I so enjoy studying after him because his knowledge of the original Hebrew sheds much light on the ancient scriptures. His quote below, and the Jewish view that earthly Jerusalem mirrors heavenly Jerusalem, helped me see more clearly the joining of the two:

> And the joy and blessedness of returned and re-deemed Israel in literal Zion will be a type and re-flection also of the even fuller joy and greater bless-edness of the ransomed of the Lord out of every nation and people and tongue [the church] —which will then be safely gathered unto Him in the heaven-ly Zion, "the Jerusalem that is above," of which the literal Jerusalem will, during the millennial period, be, as it were, the earthly vestibule.[4]

My minibook, *Jerusalem: Above and Below,*[5] goes into the subject in more detail.

However, I will point out here another interesting fact. When Jewish Israelis pronounce the name of the city, they say *Yerushalayim.*

The number *two* in Hebrew is *shta-im.* But you don't need to say *shta-im* before items that come in pairs. You simply put the double ending on the word itself. For instance, notice the dual ending to words indicating things that come in twos: *mishkafayim* (eyeglasses), *na'alayim* (shoes), *yad'ayim* (hands).

Yerushalayim has a dual ending indicating there are two.

Therefore when we pray

> *Yerushalayim has a duel ending indicating there are two.*

for the *peace* of Jerusalem, we are praying for its *wholeness*. We are praying for the earthly city to remain the undivided and eternal capital of Israel. And we are praying for the coming together of the upper and lower cities in God's wonderful plan that they be "builded together."

WHAT SHALL BE THE DURATION OF OUR PRAYING?

Isaiah 62:1-4 is the Messiah's intercession for Israel and Jerusalem. Then follows the fact that the Lord has set "watchmen" upon the walls of Jerusalem to join in that intercession (vv 6, 7.)

> **KJV**
> **Is. 62:6** I have set watchmen upon thy walls, O Jerusalem, *which* shall never hold their peace day nor night: ye that make mention of the LORD, keep not silence,
> **Is. 62:7** And give him no rest, till he establish, and till he make Jerusalem a praise in the earth.

My King James Bible is a reference Bible. A marginal note to the phrase, "ye that make mention of the LORD" gives the literal Hebrew as, *"you who are the LORD's remembrancers."* Another marginal reference notes that the word translated *rest* in verse 7 is literally *silence*. Again, Young's is more accurate:

> **Young's Literal Translation**
> **Is. 62:6** 'On thy walls, O Jerusalem, I have appointed watchmen, All the day, and all the night, Continually, they are not silent.' O ye remembrancers of Jehovah, Keep not silence for yourselves,
> **Is. 62:7** And give not silence to Him, Till He establish, and till He make Jerusalem A praise in the earth.

David Baron says that the remembrancers of Jehovah are those who remind Him of what is yet to be done, "of what I still am, and I may be expected to do."[6] In other words, these remembrancers are to bring up God's Word regarding His promises for Jerusalem.

These watchmen are to "give Him no silence." Their uttering of His Word is to be declared into the earth continually. And thereby, He can clothe the proclaimed prophecies with fulfillment.

> *Such prayers are to be made until His promises are fully fulfilled.*

Such prayers are to be made until His promises are fully fulfilled.

Until He has established Jerusalem a praise in the earth.

PRAYING THE MYSTERY OF ISRAEL

One of the mysteries of God that the New Testament identifies is "the mystery of Israel," (Romans 11:25-26). Please see the chapter in this book, "Praying the Mysteries of God."

And even with all the above, when people ask me how to pray for Israel, I usually tell them that the best way is to pray in tongues. My advice is based on these Scriptures:

> **Rom. 8:26** Likewise the Spirit also helpeth our infirmities [singular: infirmity]: for we know not what we should pray for as we ought: but the Spirit itself (Himself) maketh intercession for us with groanings which cannot be uttered.

Rom. 8:27 And he that searcheth the hearts knoweth what *is* the mind of the Spirit, because he maketh intercession for the saints according to *the will of* God.

1 Cor. 14:2 For he that speaketh in an *unknown* tongue speaketh not unto men, but unto God: for no man understandeth *him;* howbeit in the spirit he speaketh mysteries...

1 Cor. 14:14 For if I pray in an *unknown* tongue, my spirit prayeth, but my understanding is unfruitful.
1 Cor. 14:15 What is it then? I will pray with the spirit, and I will pray with the understanding also: I will sing with the spirit, and I will sing with the understanding also.

---

1. David Baron, *Israel in the Plan of God,* (Grand Rapids, MI: Kregel Publications, 1983), p 50.

2. Dr. Billye Brim, *Judgment of the Nations for How They Treat Israel,* Billye Brim Ministries, P.O. Box 40, Branson, MO 65615. 2013.

3. Edward Horowitz, M.A., D.R.E., *HOW THE HEBREW LANGUAGE GREW,* KTAV Publishing House Inc., Jersey City, NJ. 1960, pp 22, 27, 46, 47.

4. David Baron, *Israel in the Plan of God,* Kregel Publications, Grand Rapids, MI 49501, 1983, pp 301, 302.

5. Dr, Billye Brim, *JERUSALEM, Above and Below,* Billye Brim Ministries, P. O. Box 40, Branson, MO 65615. 2014.

6. David Baron, *Types, Psalms, and Prophecies,* Keren Ahvah Meshihit, P.O. Box 10382, 91103 Jerusalem, Israel. 2013, p52.

CHAPTER 24

FELLOWSHIPPING WITH THE FATHER

Effective prayer is increased a thousand fold when the pray-er knows the Father—when that pray-er has a personal prayer life and communion with the Father. I knew there had to be a chapter on fellowshipping with Him. And I gave the assignment to my 24-year-old granddaughter, Hannah. Why? Because I know she does it. She fellowships with the Father. She knows Him. And she started as a little girl. I also wanted to show that prayer is not just for "older folk." —*Billye Brim*

Fellowshipping With The Father
by
Hannah Brim

There is a difference between fellowship and relationship. Fellowship is when you spend time with someone. You know their voice when they call you on the phone because you've spent time with that person. You've shared interests with that person. Relationship is when you are connected to someone by blood, or through a marriage. You may have a relationship with someone, but because you haven't fellowshipped with that person, you don't know anything about him or her. Someone may have asked Jesus into his or her heart, but never really fellowshipped with God. That person is related to God through the blood of Jesus and they will go to Heaven. But they haven't really experienced the depth of getting to know God on a personal level. I personally believe God is wanting us to know Him on a personal level, as Father; and one of the ways we get to know His heart is through fellowshipping with Him in prayer.

I remember when I was six-years-old, lying on my bed looking up at the ceiling, and telling God about my day. I would talk to God just like I would talk to my best friend. I would tell Him about my school day—what happened in class, what I had for lunch that day, and other times whatever I could tell Him off the top of my head.

Sometimes I would tell God my cares and ask for His help.

One time in particular, in my talks with God, I was telling Him that all the kids would get picked up after school by their mom and dad. My parents divorced when I was about two. I knew that something was different, as I compared myself with other classmates.

While I was talking to the Lord, I could sense a warm sweet Presence down inside of me. Then this thought came to me *that I could ask God to be my Father!* When I told the Lord that I wanted Him to be my Father, I could sense His love encompass my heart, and I knew that everything was going to be Ok. As I grew older, I realized it was the sweet Presence of the Holy Spirit leading me to let God be my Father in my life!

HEART-FELT PRAYING

When God does something, I believe He does it with a purpose. Likewise when we pray, we should pray with a purpose. You can pray with purpose in the Spirit without knowing mentally what you're praying about.

Elijah was a man of God and he is given as an example of praying with purpose (James 5:17, 18). The very next verse says, "The earnest (heartfelt, continued) prayer of a righteous man makes tremendous power available [dynamic in its working]" (James 5:16 AMP).

We pray with purpose by praying from our heart. Heart-felt prayers are the most powerful prayers because they come from your heart. When you fellowship and spend time with God you will get to know His heart, and begin to pray out His heart.

I believe as we spend time and commune with God that His desires and our desires start to become one. *"Delight yourself also in the LORD, and He shall give you the desires of your heart"* (Psalm 37:4). So whatever God's desires are will become our desires because we've spent time with Him and communed with Him through prayer.

THE HELPER

The Holy Spirit reveals to us the character of the Father. When we spend time with Him and commune with Him we will know Him in an intimate way.

"And I will pray the Father, and He will give you another Helper, that He may abide with you forever—the Spirit

204 How You Can Pray in the End of Days

of truth, whom the world cannot receive, because it neither sees Him nor knows Him: but you know Him; for He dwells with you and will be in you" (John 14:16-17 NKJV).

Jesus prayed to the Father, and so we are to pray to the Father. New Covenant prayer is to the Father in the Name of the Son (John 16:23, 24).

Jesus prayed that God would send us the Holy Spirit who would be a help to us. Scripture says that we know Him because He lives inside of us. The Holy Spirit is to reveal to us who the Father is. I believe we are to fellowship, and acknowledge the Holy Spirit in our lives, if we want to pray on a deeper level. I personally like to talk to Him throughout my day. I ask Him frequently to help me find things, mainly my car keys!

One very dark night as I was getting out of my car, I tripped and dropped my purse. I didn't realize that my keys fell out into a pile of leaves. The next day my brother asked me if he could drive my car, so I started looking. *Where did I put my keys?* I looked in my purse. I searched everywhere. Panic tried to set in.

I decided to stop searching. I asked the Holy Spirit, the Spirit of Truth, to reveal to me where I put my keys. I started praying in the Spirit. Suddenly, I saw an image of a pile of leaves. I stopped praying and thought, *Why am I praying about leaves?* It sounded strange to my mind. (A lot of times when we try to figure out what we are praying about, to our minds it seems strange. That's why it is important that we trust the Holy Spirit.) I had a leading to go outside and look at the pile of leaves right by my car. I walked outside and saw my keys buried in the pile of leaves. I was so overwhelmed with joy! The Holy Spirit had helped me find them! My faith was encouraged!

In my daily life, I have noticed, the more I yield to the Holy Spirit, it becomes easier to know when He needs me to pray about something. I begin to get comfortable with His leadings—I know when He needs me to pray. When you do this you will no longer feel alone, because you will be more aware of His Presence inside of you. He will become your best friend.

You can tell when someone spends time in the Presence of God. It almost seems like there is a light on them.

In First John 1:3 (AMP) it says, "What we have seen and [ourselves] heard we are also telling you, so that you too may realize and enjoy fellowship as partners and partakers with us. And [this] fellowship that we have [which is a distinguishing mark of Christians] is with the Father and with His Son Jesus Christ (the Messiah)."

When something is *marked* there is an impression upon it. A police car is *marked.* It is different than all the rest of the cars. That's the way it is with us when we fellowship with God, and spend time in His Presence. God's Presence will mark you. He will make an impression upon you; and you will stand out from the world.

IT'S TIME TO KNOW GOD

When I graduated from high school I sensed that the Lord was leading me to attend *Rhema Bible Training Center.* I remember the car ride from Branson, Missouri to Tulsa, Oklahoma. I was driving my little white Prius (named the Baby Car) that was jammed packed with things for my apartment. I cried the first couple hours of the trip (leaving my family, and everything I was familiar with). But even as I was crying, I had such a peace down on the inside of me that kept me stable. I knew it was the great Comforter, the Holy Spirit.

My roommate asked me to go to *Rhema's Prayer School* with her one afternoon. Having been brought up in a praying family, I loved to pray. So I looked forward to going.

As the students began filling the room, there was such expectancy in the air. I listened intently to *Rhema's* Prayer and Healing Coordinator, Leigh Ann Soesbee (aka 'Miss Leigh Ann' to the students).

Suddenly, she paused mid-sentence and pointed her finger, "Everyone in this section [mine] who wants prayer come down to the front."

My friend and I walked down to the front as fast as we could. As Miss Leigh Ann was praying, she turned, and looked over to me, and said by the Spirit, "It's time for you to know God for who He is to you personally."

I didn't fully comprehend what those words meant; but as time unfolded the more understanding I have of them. I knew that I was going to have to know God for who He was to me, in every area of my life. My grandmother had all these wonderful experiences with God, but now it was time for me to experience Him in a more intimate way. God wants all of us, spirit, soul, and body (1 Thess 5:23). He wanted me to let Him in, in every area of my life!

Preparing The Way

I believe that part of the role of the Body of Christ is to prepare the way of the Lord. As we yield to the Holy Spirit through prayer, we will make way for His Second Coming (both His appearing in the rapture, and when He physically returns).

Just like John was a "voice" to the first coming, we are to use our "voices" in prayer to make way for His Second Coming.

Concerning John the Baptist, the Word says, "And you, child, will be called the prophet of the Highest; For you will go before the face of the LORD to prepare His ways" (Luke 1:76 NKJV).

And it is written, "Behold, I will send you Elijah the prophet before the coming of the great and dreadful day of the LORD. And he will turn the hearts of the fathers to the children, And the hearts of the children to their fathers... (Mal 4:5-6 NKJV).

Before Jesus comes back for His bride, there is to be a restoration with our hearts towards our Heavenly Father. God is stirring our hearts back to Him. To know Him as our Heavenly Father in a more intimate way than we have ever known before this time. To know His love. He is calling us (spirit, soul, and body) to higher and higher intimate places—to work with Him, and in Him.

Throughout my life, I have met a lot of wonderful people, but God has placed only a handful of friends whom I refer to as my "heart friends." They are the friends that I share my heart to, and I trust them.

God wants us to share our hearts to Him, and He wants to share His heart with you! Before Jesus comes back there will be a greater depth of intimacy with our Heavenly Father. He is inviting us to spend time with Him, and speak to Him in a more personal way. Our purpose should be just like Paul's "That I may know Him [intimately] and the power of His resurrection..." (Phil 3:10 NKJV).

I believe as you're reading this, He is knocking at the door of your heart right now. I hear Him saying, *Let me in those places in your life to heal you, and restore you. My plans for you are good and just!*

Hannah Brim is a graduate of *Rhema Bible Training Center*. After graduation she assisted in the *Prayer and Healing School* there for two years. Then she became the personal travel companion to her grandmother, Dr. Billye Brim. Her heart is for the younger generation to know communion with God, and how to work with Him in prayer. To that end, she teaches a monthly session from *Prayer Mountain in the Ozarks* that is streamed live, and also archived. She writes for her web page called *"Hannah's Prayers."*

(Hannah won't like my saying this, but I am doing it because I want you to see that she is an all around person. And not "monk-like." She was an outstanding basketball player. And in the two years she played at Rhema, they were back-to-back National Champions. She was named an All American. —*Billye Brim*)

A Tent Meeting in Coweta

Back side of picture: I like the way she identified these people in the early days of Pentecost - "Penacostal People."

L to R:
Carrie Pickard and Mr. & Mrs. George Snelson

My Great Grandma (Carrie) Pickard

L to R: Isaac Pickard and William Isaac Combs

William F. Combs and Nannie Pickard (my grandparents), just before their marriage.

Wedding of Nannie Pickard and William F. Combs at the
Pickard Place South of Coweta

L to R, Second from Left: Levi Pickard, Lou Pipes Pickard, Carrie Pipes
Pickard, Ike Pickard (their son between them).

Nannie Pickard Combs
and "Little Willie"

My parents, Willie
and Marie Combs

Daddy's Girl
Billye Marie (10 mo.)

Our Senior
pictures -
Kent Brim
and I were
high school
sweethearts.

Our children the year I met
Kenneth E. Hagin - 1967.
Shelli (9-1/2) - Brenda (6)
Terry (8) - Chip (4)

Below
My Family - at The Combs'
on the Lake. (circa 1976)

Back row, L to R: Kent, Terry, & Billye Brim, Willie Combs,
Don & Pat Whitenack.
Front row, L to R:
Brenda Brim, Donna
& Gayla Whitenack,
Marie Combs,
Chip & Shelli Brim.

Hannah Brim,
with her
PaPa Combs

A staff photo taken during my time as Editor at Kenneth Hagin Ministries.

Editor Billye Brim (seated) with Associate Editor Phyllis Mackall (center) and transcribers Fran Kerce (left) and Berta Bass.

Rhema Fall Bible Seminar 1985

Above: Patsy (Behr-man) Cameneti, Billye Brim, Phil Halverson, & Kenneth E. Hagin

Left: Jeanne Wilkerson & Kenneth E. Hagin

**I answered
the call
to preach.**

Phil & Fern
Halverson

Wilford &
Gertrude Reidt

Rev. J.R. & Carmen Goodwin

Rachel Teafatiller

Painting of
the two
Jerusalems.
Painting by
Bracha Brym-Lavee.

An oil painting of
Shulamith
Katznelson
and Billye Brim
by Shelli Jones.

We visited with
Prime Minister
Ariel Sharon,
several times
over the years.

214

Reading Psalm 33:10
to Prime Minister
Ariel Sharon,
September 11, 2000.

Sharon at the
Western Wall
Sept. 28, 2000.

Billye Brim, Mayor Ron
Nachman, builder of Ariel
(upper right), & Prime
Minister Benyamin
Netanyahu (seated).

**We take
seminar
teaching
tours to Israel
every year.**

Planting grape vines
in *the Land.*

Teaching on the
Southern Steps
in Jerusalem.

Prayer Mountain in the Ozarks

The Administration Building houses the ministry offices, prayer chapel, and a bookstore.

The Pickard Place, is our largest with 3 bedrooms, a full kitchen & great room.

Halverson House, sleeps 4 and has a cozy atmosphere for intimate time with the Lord.

Uncle Joe's Cabin also sleeps 4 and has a loft bedroom which looks down on the stone fireplace and kitchen.

The prayer group at *Prayer Mountain* before the Chapel was finished. (Circa 1999)

Wednesday Noon Prayer Webcast from the Chapel at *Prayer Mountain.*

Each fall we hold the *Autumn Assembly of Prayer* in Branson, Missouri.

Tent Meeting on *Prayer Mountain*

BIBLIOGRAPHY

Ariel, Gidon and O'Dell, Bob. BLOOD MOONS 101. Root Source. (http://root-source.com/blood-moons-101)

Baron, David. *Israel in the Plan of God.* Kregel Publications, Grand Rapids, MI. 1983.

Baron, David. *Types, Psalms and Prophecies.* Keren Ahvah Meshi-hit, Jerusalem, Israel.

Biltz, Mark. *Blood Moons.* WND Books, Washington, D.C.

Brim, Dr. Billye. *Judgment of the Nations for How They Treat Israel.* Billye Brim Ministries, Branson, MO.

Brim, Dr. Billye. *JERUSALEM, Above and Below.* Billye Brim Ministries, Branson, MO.

Brim, Dr. Billye. *Letters to Partners in the Service of the Lord.* Billye Brim Ministries, Branson, MO.

Brim, Dr. Billye. *The Blood and the Glory.* Harrison House, Tulsa, OK.

Brim, Dr. Billye. *The Book of Daniel, Syllabus.*

Brim, Dr. Billye. *The Book of Revelation, Syllabus.*

Hagee, John. *Four Blood Moons, Something is About to Change.* Worthy Publishing, Brentwood, TN.

Hagin, Kenneth E. *I Believe in Visions.* RHEMA BIBLE CHURCH, aka Kenneth Hagin Ministries, Inc., Tulsa, OK.

Bible Prayer Study Course.
TONGUES BEYOND THE UPPER ROOM.
Prevailing Prayer to Peace.
The Believer's Authority.

Halverson, Phillip and Fern. *Unseen Forces Beyond This World.* Harrison House, Tulsa OK.

Horowitz, Edward. *HOW THE HEBREW LANGUAGE GREW.* KTAV Publishing House, Inc., Jersey City, NJ. 1988.

Lake, John G. *John G. Lake, His Life, His sermons, His Boldness of Faith.* Kenneth Copeland Publications, Ft. Worth, TX.

MacMillan, John A. *The Authority of the Believer.* Wing Spread Publishers, Camp Hill, PA.

Shakarian, Demos, as told to John and Elizabeth Sherrill. *The Happiest People on Earth.* Fleming H. Revell. 1979.

Sherrill, John. *They Speak With Other Tongues.* CHOSEN, a division of Baker Publishing Group, Minneapolis, MN.

Seymore, William J. *The Azusa Street Papers.* [A Reprint of: *The Apostolic Faith Mission Publications* (1906-1908). William J. Seymore, Editor.] Harvest Publications, Foley, AL.

BIBLES

American Standard Version
Amplified
God's Word
King James Version
Moffatt's

ArtScroll Tanach Series, Mesorah Publications, Ltd.
    Chumash, The Stone Edition.
    Daniel, The Book of Daniel.
    Trei Asar, The Twelve Prophets.
    Yechezkel, The Book of Ezekiel.

Ne'am Lo'ez, Moznaim Publishing Corporation, New York/Jerusalem.*Yirmeyahu, The Book of Jeremiah.*

The Companion Bible. With Notes and Appendixes by E. W. Bullinger. Kregal Publications, Grand Rapids, MI.

About the Author

Billye Brim's Christian heritage is rich. She sensed the call of God in early childhood. However, it was only after an encounter with the Holy Spirit in 1967, that she as a young wife and mother of four began to follow Him to walk out her call. For almost ten years she served as Editor of Publications for Kenneth E. Hagin Ministries where she also taught at Rhema Bible Training Center.

Immediately after ordination in 1980 she traveled to Soviet Russia in what proved to be ongoing ministry there. Since then she has literally ministered around the world several times over.

Kent and Billye Brim with Lee and Jan Morgans founded a local church in Collinsville, Oklahoma. A Glorious Church Fellowship is the foundation of Billye Brim Ministries and Prayer Mountain in the Ozarks in Branson, Missouri, and the soon-to-be-built Migdal Arbel Prayer and Study Center in Israel.

When Kent passed away in 1986, Billye was led to "study Hebrew in the Land." Studying at Ulpan Akiva in Israel led to the unique Seminar Tours she has guided in the Land from 1986 to now. It also provided a pattern for the Prayer and

Study Center in Israel.

"Helping Pray-ers" is a God-given directive in her life. One place this happens is at Prayer Mountain in the Ozarks near Branson, Missouri. On 300 plus acres, log cabins provide places for individual prayer, or small prayer groups. Corporate prayer meetings are held twice a week in the chapel.

On Wednesdays at 12 Noon CST, the meeting is streamed live. Pray-ers, who have named themselves World-Wide Pray-ers (WWPs), join in united prayer via thousands of computers in more than 60 nations. This prayer is focused primarily on an Awakening to God. For in a corporate prayer meeting in June 2008, Billye Brim and the pray-ers were impressed with these words: *One thing will save America...an Awakening to God. One thing will avail for Israel and the nations, An Awakening to God.*

She also hosts an *Autumn Assembly of Prayer* in Branson each fall, where several thousand pray-ers from around the world gather.

First Corinthians 10:32 is foundational in Billye Brim's ministry. The "good works that He has ordained that she should walk in" involve activity among the Jews, the Nations, and the Church—all to the Glory of God.